RIHANNA

REBEL FLOWER

RIHA

NNA

REBEL FLOWER

CHLOE GOVAN

OMNIBUS PRESS

London / New York / Paris / Sydney / Copenhagen / Berlin / Madrid / Tokyo

Exclusive Distributors
Music Sales Limited,
14/15 Berners Street,
London, W1T 3LJ.

Music Sales Corporation,
257 Park Avenue South,
New York, NY 10010, USA.

Macmillan Distribution Services,
56 Parkwest Drive
Derrimut, Vic 3030,
Australia.

Every effort has been made to trace the copyright holders of the photographs in this book but one
or two were unreachable. We would be grateful if the photographers concerned would contact us.

Typeset by Phoenix Photosetting, Chatham, Kent
Printed in the EU

A catalogue record for this book is available from the British Library.

Visit Omnibus Press on the web at www.omnibuspress.com

Contents

Chapter 1

Growing Pains

Forget sugarcane – Rihanna is Barbados' biggest export, with sales of over 15 million albums worldwide. Officially the highest charting and most successful Bajan – that is, Barbadian – artist of all time, the small-town girl with obscenely big dreams broke out of her island idyll to become a global superstar. But where did it all begin for the girl who, since childhood, had found herself blessed with the nickname Rebel Flower?

Rihanna grew up on what to many seems the ultimate paradise island, where turquoise blue waves lapped at infinite sandy beaches, where postcard-perfect coastline stretched as far as the eye could see, where the sun was always shining, and where – even at night – temperatures barely dipped below 25°C.

But the sun was rarely shining in Rihanna's heart. Beneath the paradise mirage was a life of dark secrets, harsh betrayal, drug abuse, brutal violence and never-ending heartache.

She had been brought into the world by Monica and Ronald Fenty, both immigrants to Barbados. Ronald's ancestors had been Irish settlers on the losing side of the vicious English Civil War of the 1600s and, consequently, had been exiled to the island to become indentured servants.

In an act of defiance, some immigrants allegedly married their own brothers and sisters in a bid to keep their bloodlines pure. They resented their new lives of servitude at the mercy of wealthy plantation owners and exploitative employers. They might have stood out as being pale-skinned newcomers to the island, when back in Ireland barely a lick of sunshine had touched their faces, but there was one thing they had in common with the locals – a hatred of powerful companies and the pitifully low wages they provided.

Even worse, throughout the 1900s many people were escaping the country due to high rates of unemployment and poverty. Refusing to be beaten, Ronald's ancestors did the opposite and stayed put.

Their saving grace turned out to be tourism. Being surrounded by wealthy holidaymakers who had come with only fun in mind – a hedonistic weekend of sun, sea and sand – might have made the local Bajan workers resentful; but it was the exotic appeal of Barbadian shores that had saved the island's flagging economy. Hospitality quickly surpassed sugarcane to become the top source of income in the country, and, eventually, one in every five Bajan residents would be employed in the tourist trade, some of Ronald's relatives included.

Rihanna's mother was also an immigrant, hailing from the little-known British colony of Guyana – a beautiful land of reefs and rainforests nestled just north of Brazil and a little east of Venezuela. She had shared her South American heritage with an African–American mother who had moved to Barbados soon after she was born.

Finding herself on Barbados, Monica met Ronald when the two were high-school students. There was an instant attraction, but it wasn't plain sailing. By the age of 14, Ronald had already discovered the temptations of marijuana and crack cocaine. However, Monica was undeterred. The two became firm friends and, later, lovers.

They married in 1985, by which time the two were both in their thirties, but their marriage was ill-fated from the start. Back then, less than two percent of marriages had been 'mulatto' – mixed race – and such relationships were often taboo for social and political reasons. Behind the scenes many mixed-race couples were secretly sharing homes, but Rihanna's parents were among the few to come out of the closet and publicly declare their love for one another through marriage. Not everyone approved, and the two had to endure the occasional stare, taunt or catty remark as commonplace – but that was the least of their worries.

By now, Ronald had developed a severe drug addiction. If Monica had hoped she could change his ways, she had been sorely mistaken. As much as he wanted to quit, substance abuse had now taken over his life. The newly-weds lived together in Bridgetown, which, despite being the island's capital, was a small, tight-knit community and Ronald soon built up a reputation as a *parrow* – Barbadian slang for a 'scrounging junkie'.

In fact, rumours were even rife that his drug abuse had left him infertile, accounting for the couple's initially childless marriage. The gossipmongers were proved wrong on February 20, 1988 when the couple's first daughter was born – Robyn Rihanna Fenty.

Finding it difficult to deal with the upheaval of the new arrival, Ronald would flee the family home for days at a time on cocaine binges, leaving his wife to take care of the newborn. While her father was scoring crack and her mother was working all the hours that God sent to keep the family finances in check, Rihanna was distracting herself in a very different way – by singing. At age three, she would stand in front of her bedroom mirror, an imaginary microphone or her mother's hairbrush clasped in her hands, singing the words to Whitney Houston's 'Saving All My Love For You'. What was more, as soon as she was able to walk, she also mastered the dance routines.

Singing and performing were essential diversions for Rihanna as she dodged her parents' increasingly ferocious battles. "Even as a child, I would learn that my mom and dad would argue when there was foil paper in the ashtray," she later told *The Mirror*.

There was also prolific violence – on one occasion, Ronald even broke his wife's nose in front of her. Rihanna would cling onto his legs and smash glasses in a desperate attempt to save her mother and distract her father from the beatings. "I was out of control," Ronald acknowledged to *The Sun*. "I would let my wife and children down time and time again. I was not a good dad or husband."

Rihanna agreed, telling *The Observer*, "A child shouldn't have to go through that. Being in the whirlwind, it frustrates you, it angers you, because you're being tortured and you don't know why."

Over the years, suffering from an abusive father, she continued to find refuge in song. She was inspired by the tunes that blared out from the reggae nightclub her mother ran at the time, and became a huge fan of artists such as Bob Marley. Uplifting songs such as 'No Woman, No Cry', which made the best out of a bad situation, lifted her out of her depression.

It was almost compulsory for a young Bajan girl to listen to copious amounts of reggae; but, going against the grain, the young Rihanna – still known to everyone by her first name, Robyn – also sought out a more balanced musical diet as she grew up. This included Shaggy, Diana Ross and Mariah Carey.

"Reggae wasn't enough for Robyn anymore," a childhood friend told the author. "She was frustrated by how local sega or reggae artists weren't getting much success outside of Bridgetown. She started to look up to the American artists more because they were given more recognition and they'd made their dreams come true. They were pulling audiences from all around the world. Actually, the girls at school dissed her for turning her back on our local culture, thinking she was better than the rest."

And music wasn't the only reason she was singled out for abuse at school. Rihanna had always stood out as different, due to her unusually light skin and green eyes, and at primary school, she was bullied relentlessly and told that she was "an ugly pig".

But music dominated Rihanna's life: whether it was Bob Marley, Destiny's Child or an obscure sega group from back home adorning her playlist, Rihanna would sing along – and loud. She would sing in the school cafeteria, on the beach, on balconies or even at home in the shower. The latter caused her some trouble at times. Her neighbours might have been embarrassed to mention the near daily arguments, physical fights and piercing screams they heard echoing through the perilously thin walls of her home – domestic violence was another taboo – but they were less restrained when it came to criticising Rihanna's singing.

"We used to call her Robyn Red Breast," joked her long-time neighbour Dawn Johnson to *The Sun*. "She was always singing like a bird. We are so close we could hear her singing from the bathroom."

Although Dawn had remembered her voice with affection, others hadn't been nearly as kind. Rihanna's childhood friend continued: "People would actually taunt her, she would get told to shut up, and they barely stopped short of complaining to her folks. I don't know if she'd like me telling you this, but she was in tears over it more than once. Singing should be natural, but she was made to feel uncomfortable and forced to cover it up – like she had to hold herself in. It wasn't just her father who clipped her wings."

Her father might have been unpredictable, suffering from drug-related mood swings, but – in a twist of fate – music turned out to be the one thing they could bond over. Aged seven, Rihanna's voice came to his attention, burning through his consciousness, as she belted out 'A Whole New World', a song from the *Aladdin* soundtrack. "I was in the lounge and heard this angelic singing from the balcony," he told *The Sun*. "I looked out and it was Rihanna. My heart jumped. I knew then she was special."

Believing she had inherited her singing talent from his parents, Ronald began to pay more attention to her and the two grew closer. "I still vividly remember all the good things, like playing with him on the beach and catching crabs," Rihanna told *The Mirror* of that time. Her father's drug use also seemed to have subsided. But underneath these brief moments of happiness, a storm was brewing. She had his love and approval for now – but for how much longer?

Before long, the wheel of fortune dipped down again in her life. Even discovering who was responsible for Rihanna's talent became a bone of contention. "Her mum says Robyn takes after her, but I know the singing is definitely from me," Ronald told *The Mirror* in defiance. Both of his parents had been keen singers, sometimes performing professionally.

By now, Ronald had left his job as a warehouse supervisor and had taken on the role of a full-time house husband as Monica struggled to support the family on her own meagre wages. Rihanna began to see more of him – and she realised she didn't always much like what she saw.

"I had seen the marijuana around him, but I didn't know what it was," she recalled to *The Daily Mail*. "I just know that my mum didn't like it and they were always fighting about it. My mother was a very strong woman and tried to shelter us from it as much as she could. But she was working and he was at home, so there was only so much she could hide from us."

As the fighting escalated yet again, Rihanna would sit on the stairs, her eyes closed and her fists clenched, muttering, "I'll never date someone like my dad – never!" over and over as tears streamed silently down her face. When her father was coming down from a hit, he could become enraged even by the sound of someone crying – so she had learnt to keep her grief under cover. Living in constant fear of more attacks, the last thing she wanted to do was trigger her father's violence.

What was more, in Barbadian culture, airing one's dirty laundry in public was frowned upon – and something as controversial as violence had to be kept a closely guarded secret. "In Barbados we don't [talk about abuse]. We keep it in our family and figure it out and move on," Rihanna revealed matter-of-factly to *The Observer*. She added, "Domestic violence is a big secret. No kid goes around and lets people know that their parents fight."

But it was becoming harder and harder to keep her feelings in check. Her betrayed mother would even make snide remarks as they passed homeless men in the street. "We were walking down the street with the kids and there was a guy sleeping on the sidewalk," Ronald recalled to *The Sun*. "Her mother said to Robyn, 'Your dad is going to end up like that.' I did not want my children to see me sleeping on the sidewalk, so I started making the changes." However, his addiction was ruling his life and it was too little, too late.

At the age of nine, Rihanna unwittingly triggered her parents' separation, when she caught her father in the act. It wasn't simply tell-tale foil wrappers in the ashtray that caught her eye this time, but her father with a crack pipe locked to his lips. He had promised his wife that he would quit drugs but – even as an innocent child – Rihanna knew better. Fearfully spying on her father through a crack in the kitchen door, she decided she had to do something. It was a tough call for

Rihanna but – knowing how it upset her mother – she knew she had to be honest and confide in her about what she had seen. Within days, Ronald had left the family home.

"I just know that my mom and dad would always fight if there was a foil paper in the ashtray," Rihanna recalled to *Giant* of that time. "He would just go to the bathroom all the time. I didn't know what it was. I really did not know. I just thought it was normal. Then he did it again and I told her. I said, 'Mom, he did that ashtray thing again…'"

The guilt of being found out by his daughter brought Ronald back down to earth with a crash. He told *The Sun,* "I turned and looked Rihanna in the eye and instantly came back down from the high I was on. I saw her run for her mother, ask her something and then they both started to cry. I had no idea she had been watching. It was the lowest point – life just stopped and I realised what a fool I had been."

Monica was furious that her daughter's innocence had been shattered at such a young age – and she resolved to kick him out of the house once and for all. There were no more second chances, no more waiting for him to kick his habit.

"It really broke her mum's heart," an close friend told the author. "She hated the thought that Robyn might come to see that as normal and one day start doing it herself."

She'd always tried to protect her from that kind of thing. She was a regular in church so I guess what he was doing went against her beliefs. But I remember Robyn feeling so guilty – she felt as if, because it was her who'd found him, that it was her fault he'd left – that if she'd just kept quiet, he would still have been at home. To her, she'd lost her father and it was all her fault. She couldn't stand it."

As she struggled to shoulder the guilt, her feelings gradually turned to anger. "I hated him," Rihanna told *The Guardian*. "Then one of my school friends who I was very close to, she knew, and she always used to say, 'You can't hate your father,' that you have to love him at the end of the day because he's your father. So I listened, as much as it took it out of me."

Her friend's advice led Rihanna's feelings to spiral back down into guilt. She started to question all over again whether her parents' separation had been down to her own poor judgement – crying to her mother about the crack cocaine, when, perhaps, she should have left it alone.

She began to suffer intense migraines on a daily basis, causing her mother to panic that she might have developed a brain tumour. In reality, she was simply repressing her feelings – and buckling under the stress.

"I was just taking on too much," she confessed to *Giant* magazine. "I wouldn't cry or act, so it really affected me in [my head]. I would go to school like a normal kid. No-one would know that I had a problem. I always had a smile on my face, but that's when it started to mess with me." From then on, inside, Rihanna was always crying.

What saddened her the most was that she still loved the very man who had abused her. "Some of my most memorable childhood experiences were with him," she recalled to the *Daily Mail*. "He taught me how to swim, fish and ride [a bicycle]. He's the one who made me tough and prepared me for the world."

To an outsider, rearing such a resilient daughter might have made Ronald appear to be the perfect dad – in reality, Rihanna had needed to be tough because of the misery that his drug abuse had heaped on the family. The fact that she doted on him made it even harder to accept his faults; but, feeling from that moment that she couldn't trust him to show her right from wrong, she decided to father herself.

"I think it made me very independent," she told *The Observer*. "I'm very strong... I'd always been a daddy's girl. I was daddy's girl. [Then] I found out who was doing right and who was doing wrong – and I turned into a mommy's girl."

In fact, Rihanna took her role so seriously that she became the "second mother" in the family – a surrogate parent to her younger brothers Rorrey and Rajad, born in 1989 and 1998 respectively. Ronald had nicknamed the young Rihanna 'Pinky', because of her love of feminine-coloured clothes, but she soon dispensed with the pastel pinks. It was time for her to paint on her tough-girl persona, and it was most definitely not pink.

Perhaps Rihanna was afraid of being the delicate young flower, the girly girl who dressed in pale colours, because femininity was a painful reminder of her mother, and what she had been forced to endure as she soldiered through a physically abusive relationship. Rihanna didn't want to make the same mistakes. Subconsciously, she might have wanted to shake off her archetypal female image, rejecting the pain she had seen passivity cause. Before long, her maternal grandmother was affectionately referring to her as 'Rebel Flower'.

While she was transforming herself, Rihanna also watched her mother turn from a fearful, downtrodden single mother into a strong, independent career woman determined to succeed for her family. Monica had retrained as an accountant and worked long, arduous hours of overtime, leaving Rihanna to take care of the house and the children. Yet, if it meant her sons and daughter didn't have to witness – or inhale – crack cocaine, then she felt it was a decision she had no other option but to make.

"My dad got put out of the house… because she was not having that around us," Rihanna recalled to *The Observer*. "My mom had to be a woman and a man, working her ass off for us."

At around this time, Rihanna's soundtrack to escapism was Destiny's Child, and their song 'Independent Women' struck a special chord with her. She had seen her mother fight to raise three children and to earn enough money to support the family, while also fending off the grief of losing her husband. She knew first-hand how difficult it could be, so strong female role models became prominent in her life – her mother most of all. "I was never aware that we were poor," she later told *Glamour*. "My mom never made us feel that way. She loved me unconditionally. She made us feel anything was possible and instilled in me such confidence."

However, her mother's hectic routine put a great deal of pressure on Rihanna. "[My mom] worked a lot. She was really never home – I mean, she was home, but it would be after work, late at night, so I would take care of [youngest brother Rajad]," she continued. "He was my best friend. He thought I was his mom!"

Meanwhile, Rihanna's relationship with her other brother, Rorrey, more often involved borrowing his clothes. She would put on his baggy trousers and trainers the instant she changed out of her school uniform. "I wore my brother's clothes, dresses with sneakers, or no shoes at all," she later confessed.

Her garb didn't adhere to her mother's exacting standards for a 'young lady' either. "I would always get in trouble with my mum," she continued. "She would say things to scare me, like, 'You're going to get cut!' But I couldn't help it. I would climb trees, steal mangoes, catch birds – silly things that were fun to us at the time." She was still a flower, but – like any good rose – she was also showing her thorns.

Like Katy Perry, Rihanna seemed to long to be 'one of the boys', but, despite her tomboyish persona, they weren't ready to accept her into their world. "My cousin and I were the only girls in the group," she recalled. "We would have to stand up for ourselves because the guys didn't want us around."

If her relationships with the boys were fraught, that was nothing compared to how the local girls saw her. The bullying campaign that had been waged against her stepped up even more as she grew older, leaving her infuriated. "[The prejudice] made me angry," she told *InStyle* of the taunts and catcalls she received about the colour of her skin. "It made me want to fight in my younger years. Having lighter skin wasn't a problem in my household, but it was when I went to school, which really confused me at first. For the first six years of school, I would go home traumatised. The harassment continued to my very last day of elementary school."

What was more, she didn't receive much sympathy when she chose to reveal her ordeal to the press later. "Why do you always speak so badly of the Caribbean?" a girl calling herself Shanakay raged on blog site *Out A Road*, in response to a post about Rihanna being bullied at school for her comparatively light skin colour. "You need to be proud of your roots." Another fan called Nelly added, "It's like you do not have anything positive to say about your country and your family – many Caribbean children go through it because we are of mixed nationalities, whether you're mixed with Indian, Spanish or Chinese. Stop making your life in Barbados out to be worse than it really was because we all know, Robyn – that was not the case."

Rihanna also unwittingly found herself at the centre of a race debate, with one anonymous girl insisting, "Because you were light skinned, that's why you're a star. Now you think you were the only young Bajan that could sing... It's the norm in this slavery mentality world we're still living in, so save it, Rihanna."

Rihanna's friends came to her defence. "She never thought she was better than anyone else like people are saying," one of them told the author at the time. "It's just that some girls are very sensitive about issues of race in the Caribbean. They thought that Rihanna's comments were sneering that she was superior, and they were trying to get across their own problems and their feeling of, 'Well, it's alright for *you!*'" Did lighter skinned girls really have an easier time of it? "Not necessarily, but that was the perception."

Clearly, growing up in a land of sun had been far from the idyllic childhood it might have seemed. With the combination of her pent-up aggression towards the bullies and her angst about what had been going on at home, Rihanna felt that she had the weight of the world on her shoulders. Her headaches escalated, becoming so intense that by the time she was nine she had started to black out on a regular basis.

She was admitted to hospital for a series of brain scans that would go on for years. "I wouldn't cry. I wouldn't get upset. It was all just up here, in my head," she told *Contact Music*. "I had to go through a lot of CAT scans. They even thought it was a tumour, because it was that intense. It's not great memories, but it helped to build me and make me stronger."

It wasn't an easy time for Rihanna and it was a great relief for her when she finally graduated from primary school and enrolled at Combermere, a small, mixed secondary school consisting of just 1,000 pupils.

The atmosphere in what was Barbados's oldest secondary school would prove to be a little calmer. "There was no bullying about her looks [at Combermere]," another close friend, Cheyne Jones, told the author. "That's a rumour."

Rihanna settled down and became very academic, counting maths and chemistry among her favourite subjects. She also dreamed of studying psychology at university to learn how her friends, enemies and, of course, frenemies, operated.

"I've always had a thing for reading people," she told *The Observer*. "When I come into contact with a situation or a person, the first thing I do is, I'm just quiet for a little while. I sit, I watch you, I observe you – and being able to read people helps me to know how easy it is to be read. I know the key things that show people who you are… people are shallow, they're dishonest. You can't trust them. [Psychology] really helps me to understand how to play the game."

Yet psychology was just a back-up plan – deep down, she knew she wanted to sing for a living. While she fantasised about becoming a star, she supplemented her family's meagre income by becoming a market-stall trader, using her father's bric-a-brac business for inspiration.

"She used to sell stuff on the side of the street like I did," her father, Ronald, revealed to *The Sun*. "She'd come outside of the store, put up a rack and sell hats and scarves. She would also buy sweets, put them in packages and take them to school to sell to her friends for a profit."

Assuming she would grow up to be an entrepreneur, he was shocked to learn just how serious singing had become for her. "She liked to dance and had natural rhythm, but she wasn't doing all the school productions and stuff so it came a bit out of the blue," he recalled.

Although her father had his heart set on her becoming a businesswoman and hadn't seen success coming musically, Rihanna knew exactly where she wanted to be. "I just developed a passion, singing and listening to the radio all the time. It became a dream of mine to become a singer myself," she told *The Guardian*. "I aspired to be like Mariah Carey. I wanted to make music the world would love."

However there was a setback on her journey. Her estranged father had rejoined the family, promising to kick his drug habit for good; it was too late to save the marriage, and he and Monica would finally divorce when Rihanna was 16. For the moment, however, Rihanna was delighted to have him back around the house, although she still lived in constant fear of another argument. She desperately needed a distraction, an outlet for all of the tension – so, aged 12, she decided to enrol in the summer camp run by the Barbados Cadet Corps.

It was an ideal outlet through which to channel all of her anxiety and aggression. According to popular belief, it was one of the toughest youth courses in the Caribbean, if not the world. As the founders of the camp warned, "The programme is deliberately intense, the timings will be strictly adhered to and standards will be set very high."

The rigorous training programme included a survival camp test, where cadets were challenged to pitch their own tents in the wilderness and cook food over an open fire. Their physical fitness would be tested with regular swimming, cycling and running races. But the biggest endurance test for most cadets, however, was the orienteering challenge, which involved route planning, scrambling over rough terrain and map-reading on the move. To make matters worse, the cadets would be timed on how fast they could find their feet. A mixed group of boys and girls would also take part in shooting practice with a .177 air rifle.

However, as a friend recalls, Rihanna had no trouble at all adapting to the challenges of being a cadet. "Robyn was a really smart girl," she told the author. "People thought her best friend Sonita would be the successful one, because she was planning to study medicine and she worked super hard at school. Not only was Robyn a bit of a party girl but she was seen by some people as just another pretty girl with no brains. People dismissed her as being empty-headed, but that wasn't the case at all."

She added, "She was brilliant at map reading – and imagine this gorgeous girl with model looks who would turn round and blow your mind by doing shooting practice with more precision than any guy you'd ever seen. She definitely didn't conform to what was expected of her, even then."

However, Rihanna struggled to accept her role in the cadet hierarchy. As a lowly junior cadet, she had to obey the orders of girls who had a more experienced ranking. She would be at their mercy the moment she put a foot wrong.

One such woman was the formidable Shontelle Layne – now a singer and songwriter better known simply as Shontelle – who was a drill sergeant for the team. "Picture me and Rihanna in combat boots and fatigues crawling through mud and things like that," Shontelle later told BBC Entertainment. "I had to order her around. That's what drill sergeants do. We boss cadets around, we make them do push-ups – especially when they show up on the parade square late."

Unfortunately for Rihanna, this happened all too often. Although Shontelle insisted she "wasn't one of the scary ones" and "didn't abuse my authority," there were consequences for a girl who dared to be late.

"I was drill sergeant on duty one day and they blew the horn and everyone was supposed to assemble on the parade square," Shontelle told *The Mirror*. "Everyone's there and then along comes Rihanna – Miss Robyn Fenty – straggling behind with a bunch of her buddies. The sergeant major was there watching so I knew I had to discipline them. I ordered them to drop and give me 10 press ups."

Yet her soft spot for Rihanna, whom she secretly adored, caused her to be a little more lenient than usual. She confessed, "If it had been someone else, they'd have had to do 50."

Shontelle believed she knew the reasons for her friend's constant tardiness – her preoccupation with her looks. She joked to *Lime* magazine, "She used to be really sharp all the time, but Rihanna is a diva now, she's always fabulous and glamorous. She was always that way, and she used to be late all the time because she was in the bathroom making sure her lip gloss was sparkly."

Rihanna was showing exactly why her grandmother had given her the pet name of Rebel Flower – she was tough, edgy and rebellious, but she was determined to make sure she looked good in the process.

"She's so funny," Shontelle continued. "She'd be like, 'I don't care if I'm in fatigues – I want to be the fliest person in here!' But since she was late, I was like 'Rihanna, do 10 push ups now!' I couldn't let it slide."

However, Rihanna's vanity came in useful for one thing – cadets were awarded extra brownie points for looking immaculate in the drill competition, which saw a third of the total points awarded for successful 'inspection of cadets and uniforms'. According to Shontelle, this was one area where Rihanna definitely made the grade. "In cadet camp, your appearance is important," she told *Hollywood Life*. "You have to have your shoes perfectly shined. Buttons, belt buckles, everything aligned. She totally was that. She was a really good cadet."

Unbeknown to each other, both budding army princesses had a passion for performance and were practising their vocals behind closed doors in their spare time. Plus, when drills were over, Rihanna's friends insisted that the roles reversed and Rihanna became the dominant one in their social circle.

"She really stood out," a friend recalls. "She was very cool and calm. I think Shontelle was actually in awe of her behind the scenes. She'd also try to be different. In cadets, everyone has to look identical, but Robyn would always find a way to stand out from the crowd, whether it was a crazy-coloured lip gloss or just her demeanour. She definitely wasn't ever going to blend in."

Indeed, Shontelle confessed to *The Mirror*, "I knew she was going to be famous, but I always thought Robyn was going to be a model or something. She's gorgeous." Rihanna had already been typecast as a typical tall, leggy catwalk model, but in spite of that she had also made a name for herself as a force to be reckoned with. Her background in cadets had certainly toughened her up. "People say, 'Oh, Rihanna… she's a Barbie,'" Shontelle continued. "No, she's not. She's the real deal."

She had proved herself by completing the strenuous summer camp, excelling at shooting practice, military precision and even three-mile runs. Yet there were also some less difficult areas to tackle. Debate was encouraged through a public-speaking contest, where cadets addressed topics such as, "Discuss the pros and cons of cultural penetration in your country," and "Discuss the impact of lifestyle diseases on youth in your country." The first question proved embarrassing for Rihanna due to her mixed-race background, with Irish ancestors in Sligo. Meanwhile, contrary to strict military training expectations, Rihanna was involved in what some conservative Barbadians might regard as a 'lifestyle disease' already. She had begun to party relentlessly from the tender age of 14.

"At 14 I'd go out and get drunk, but that's what teenage girls do in Barbados," she explained to the *Daily Mail*. "The country's pretty laid back about the legal age for drinking. But I never went over the top. I wasn't exactly in Amy Winehouse mode. I'd seen what alcohol and drugs had done to my dad, and I wasn't going to follow in his footsteps. I knew my limits when I was a kid."

She added, "If I go to a club, I go for the sounds. I go out to have fun, to dance and laugh at people fighting or dressed like whores. I might have a few drinks, but I don't get tipsy too easily. I don't ever get to the point where I want to throw up, can't stand straight or say things I'm likely to regret in the morning."

While drinking at 14 might have been tolerated on the island, some frowned upon her new lifestyle. Rihanna had regularly attended church as a child and lived among some very religious families, for whom even listening to calypso music was forbidden, but there she was drinking rum while dirty dancing to those very same beats. If it caused a stir, she was having too much fun to notice.

Her favourite club was The Boatyard, a 24-hour hotspot for both tourists and locals that was open 365 days a year. During the day, she would sample seafood lunches and go snorkelling with her friends, or sunbathe around the beachfront property. At night, however, things would hot up, with cheap cocktails and a fusion of pounding reggae, hip-hop and R&B beats. But there was a price to pay for her liberated lifestyle.

According to an acquaintance of Rihanna's, she quickly built up a reputation for promiscuity. "She was in the club underage trying to get with older guys," the source told *Media Takeout*, "but it hardly ever worked because she had horrible skin."

In fact, Rihanna already had two boyfriends. While things never became physical with either, the adrenaline rush of infidelity distracted her from her tough home life – until she eventually became too guilty to continue, and confessed.

The fling with her more serious boyfriend quickly ended, but she never stopped touring the clubs. During her tomboy phase, her friendships were almost exclusively with boys and this, combined with her constant partying, fuelled the rumours that she was sleeping around. Even Rihanna's mother became distrustful of her multiple friendships with the opposite sex. "I didn't get along with people very well," Rihanna explained to *Interview* magazine. "I got along with guys, but I hated the girls and the teachers. [That's where I got] my swag... all my friends, even if they weren't in my school, were always guys. My mother didn't understand that for a long time. There were all these different guys calling the house, and she probably had a totally different idea of what was happening."

She wasn't the only one. Rihanna found herself the victim of rumours from local girls, claiming that she was a slut who had slept with all the boys she could find. Rihanna, however, insisted that she was still a virgin. Her protective mother even banned her from leaving the house, hoping to prevent the chances of a teenage pregnancy. Rihanna's luck only changed when she befriended an older girl in school, Melissa Forde, who her mother liked and trusted.

"When Melissa arrived at school, she really stood out," Rihanna enthused to *You* magazine. "She was a black girl with blonde hair who wore make-up. She was the only girl in school who wore make-up, because we weren't allowed."

She added to *Seventeen,* "We just clicked. That was a time when I had no girlfriends at all, and neither did she. She was my first real girlfriend... I feel so comfortable when she's around. I feel like she's like my guardian angel."

Not only did her unconventional look match the mixed-race Rihanna's, but she had also introduced her to femininity. Although Rihanna's mother had once worked as a make-up artist, expertly transforming the faces of local women for a fee, she had forbidden her young daughter from experimenting with the products she loved.

To make matters worse, Rihanna had an older half-sister, Samantha, who was an aspiring model – one of three children by three different mothers from her father's troubled past – and Rihanna's mother would apply make-up to her for modelling shows. Rihanna, meanwhile, could only watch.

"I've loved make-up and dreamed of being a cover girl since I was a little girl," Rihanna later enthused. "I was fascinated watching my mother apply lip colour, blush and mascara."

The desire had been buried during her tomboy phase – not least because her mother had refused to allow Rihanna to test her collection – but Melissa was helping to reawaken it. "She would come over to my house with her older sister's magazines, and we would go through them and say, 'Hey, we could do something like that!' That's when I started to get into fashion and make-up," she remembered.

Her friendship with Melissa feminised her so much that she even dropped out of the cadets. "I was like, 'This is terrible! They are just screaming at me, I don't like this!'" she laughed, shuddering at the memory. Her parting shot was to get involved in the International Cadet Concert, where song and dance presentations were awarded with points. According to the rules, judging would be focused on "professionalism, talent, presentation and personal confidence". It was a brief appearance, but it reminded Rihanna of how much she loved to sing.

She started a group with her two music-loving friends, Kelenna Browne and Jose Blackman, called Contrast. The name was chosen because the girls had different racial backgrounds, and it was intended to symbolise the diversity of the island. The trio practised Destiny's Child and Mariah Carey songs religiously every weekend and wistfully dreamed of faraway fame and fortune.

Rihanna was becoming increasingly frustrated, however, with the lack of opportunities her country provided for becoming a singer. She loved being there, telling *Interview* magazine that her childhood "was perfect... we basically spent the entire day on the beach with summer all year around." However, she also felt that there was more to life. As much as she lived and breathed music and both looked and sounded the part, her chances of success living in small-town Barbados were a million to one. The reggae and sega scene back home was dominated by men and, in any case, Rihanna didn't want to be a success on home turf alone – she wanted global fame.

Yet the number of Bajan artists who had broken through internationally was almost zero, because most of the big-name producers lived in America. It would take more than a few rehearsals and shout-outs to local concert venues. Yet she was determined. "Seeing artists like B2K and JoJo come out at a young age really inspired me," she told *The Honolulu Advertiser*. "If all of these young teenagers could do it, I thought I could too."

Her competitive instinct heightened – not only did she want to break America, but she wanted to do it in a way that would put Barbados on the map internationally. Fortunately for her, a US-based record producer, Evan Rogers, was holidaying in Bridgetown and, as he had a local-born wife, was already attuned to the flavour of Barbadian music. Rihanna's friend Kelenna used her mother's connections to persuade a friend of Rogers' wife to hook them up with an audition.

Just two months before Rihanna's 15th birthday, her life was about to change forever. Yet little did she know that achieving the results she craved the most might force her to choose between herself and her best friend. It was the day that her dreams would be realised, but it was also the day that her heart would be broken. It was time for her big audition.

Chapter 2

Delusions of 'Glam'deur

Evan Rogers, the man who Rihanna hoped would change her life, was an established hit maker who had been on the R&B and pop scene since the 1980s. As well as achieving a number-one single with his own group, Rhythm Syndicate, he had also written for artists such as Eternal, Jessica Simpson, Christina Milian and ex-Spice Girl Emma Bunton. He also penned four songs on the Boyzone album *Where We Belong* – an effort which went six-times platinum – before writing for ★NSYNC, whose debut album had sold in excess of 10 million copies in the USA alone.

He had masterminded Christina Aguilera's career from the very beginning, and was part of the team that had plucked her from obscurity, made her songs global hits and her face a household name. He had proved that a good rhythm was the way to his heart when – just like his business-partner Carl Sturken – he had married a music-infatuated Bajan woman. This move was the beginning of his love affair with Caribbean music. Now it was just up to Contrast to show him they had the promised flavour.

Rihanna had researched his career and was already secretly hoping he could do for her what he had done for Christina Aguilera. True, Evan had never produced a reggae song for an artist before, and the string of pop ballads and soft-centred love songs he was famous for weren't necessarily to Rihanna's taste. But she was excited about meeting him – and the feeling was mutual.

He had invited Kelenna, Rihanna and Jose to his villa at the Sandy Lane Hotel, a location also favoured by Robbie Williams and Simon Cowell, for their audition. The hotel had an unrivalled reputation for being the first and last word in luxury on the island, attracting a mixture of celebrities, party girls with six-figure trust funds and music industry moguls hoping to kick back and be inspired by the latest rhythms. And Evan's villa was the biggest on the property, an elegant Palladian building offering more than 7,000 square feet of space, a private pool in the courtyard, and an almost unlimited supply of champagne.

Hailing from a modest, "slightly below average" neighbourhood herself, Rihanna had never seen such luxury. To her, this hotel was a world of unknown extravagance and decadence – although it was also one that she could see herself getting used to. The average room at the hotel had a price tag of £1,000 per night – and Evan's had cost much, much more. For this reason alone, Rihanna knew he had both the contacts and the financial backing to give any girl he chose a shot at being a star. This was her big chance.

The hotel's website claims that the residence is "the premier address in the Caribbean – a haven of tranquillity, a romantic retreat, or the perfect location for families who desire the finest holiday experience." For Rihanna, it was none of those things – her introduction to it was merely a stomach-churning experience where her heart was in her mouth, her hands were trembling and her very career depended on this one fleeting audition. She felt like the rap group So Solid Crew, who were given just 21 seconds to impress the producers, people who would make an almost instant judgement on their potential. "I was so nervous," she recalled to *The Observer*. "This was my connection to the big world that was so unreachable."

She needn't have worried though. Evan had two opportunities to hear her sing – both individually and as a group with her two friends – and he loved her performance on both occasions. He had always had a penchant for the sultry, exotic Barbadian look, and Rihanna's golden-brown tan and green eyes, combined with her other more traditionally Bajan features, made her unusually distinctive. Yet it was more than just her looks that had him mesmerised.

"The minute Rihanna walked into the room, it was like the other two girls didn't exist," Evan told *Entertainment Weekly*. "She carried herself like a star... But the killer was when she opened her mouth to sing. She was a little rough around the edges, but she had this edge to her voice."

Dressed all in pink, Rihanna had belted out Mariah Carey's 'Hero' and Destiny's Child's 'Emotion'. The timing was perfect. Evan and Carl had just formed a company together, Syndicated Rhythm Productions, and it could just be that they had found their very first signing.

"Her voice was raw but distinctive," Evan added to *Kurama* magazine, "and she wanted this career more than anything. A true star is obvious to me from the moment they walk into a room, [and] I always believed she was a star, from day one."

Unfortunately, he didn't feel the same way about her audition companions. Rihanna was filled with elation when she heard she was being invited back, this time with her mother, to discuss recording a demo – but her delight soon faded. She came back down to earth with a bang when she realised he had her in mind as a solo artist, despite the fact that she had arrived as part of a three-piece. What would she say to her friends – and, seeing their disappointment, how could she look them in the eye?

"We sang as a group and then we sang individually and Evan expressed an interest in helping me get a solo deal," Rihanna later explained to *The Observer*. "It was a really difficult place to be, because obviously I didn't want to hurt my friend's feelings. I didn't want to betray her, but it was a reality. We had auditioned together and individually, and that was it."

Yet to Kelenna in particular, who idolised the lifestyle of famous singers and had her heart set on becoming one, it was the ultimate betrayal. What was more, Rihanna didn't have much time to repair their frosty relationship. Two days after the original audition, she returned with her mother, who was told that her daughter had sufficient potential to warrant being flown to Evan's hometown of Stamford, Connecticut, to record a demo.

A shocked Monica agreed, on the condition that Rihanna stayed in school. Consequently, the first recording session was scheduled for the Christmas holidays – nearly a whole year later.

Reluctantly, Rihanna went back to Combermere and began the waiting game. "People thought Rihanna had let the success go to her head," a friend says. "But underneath it all, she was terrified. She wasn't signed yet. She was worried that in all that time until her holidays, the producer would have forgotten who she was or lost interest – or that he'd have signed someone else in her place, someone more flexible who didn't have to go to school. People were telling her to take it slow and easy – how many people get a career opportunity at 15? But she wouldn't listen. From then on, she was very interested in clothes and hairstyles to prepare herself, and she thought it was unfair that she had to stay in Barbados when she wanted to get on and take the next step in her career." And, her friend added, "From that point on, I can honestly say that she *hated* school."

Rihanna might have been at classes in body, but she was at the recording studio in spirit. However, she didn't let the grass grow under her feet for too long. Deciding that her rendition of 'Hero' by Mariah Carey was clearly a winning formula, she entered her school's annual talent and beauty pageant by singing it – and won. "She was the youngest girl to take part in a talent pageant at her high school," her father Ronald told *The Sun* admiringly. "All the other girls were 17, but she won."

She might have been competing against girls who had a couple of years extra experience in glamming themselves up, and who were a couple of years more worldly wise, but Rihanna hadn't been disheartened – and it had paid off. Perhaps it was her lack of nerves and the absence of desperation to win that had netted her the prize, allowing judges to see a serenely confident young woman in front of them.

"I kind of laughed at these stupid pageants," she breezily told the *Daily Mail* later. "But my friends at school dared me to do it, and my military training came in handy for learning how to balance books on my head for the catwalk." It was a pleasurable irony for her that the star of the show was someone who hadn't even wanted to enter.

The pageant was one of the things that persuaded her to become more feminine, along with the prospect of being in the public eye if she earned a record deal. Although Rihanna took pride in her appearance and was no stranger to a little lip-gloss, appearing in the pageant had been her first flirtation with full-on glamour. "It was very new and weird for me," Rihanna told *The Observer*. "I was a barefoot tomboy and only in high school I started getting very fussy with myself. That's when I started being very aware. But every woman has an ugly day."

The day that she won Miss Combermere – where guests were judged on their looks and strength of character – certainly wasn't one of those days. "The pageant ended at 11 p.m. and I didn't sleep until, like, 3 a.m.," Rihanna told *TMF*, her eyes widening and face lighting up at the memory. "I was so excited. I won a bouquet, a gong... everything." She also won the Miss Photogenic prize, one of the most sought-after categories of all.

However, the following morning, her happiness was soon shattered when she discovered that most of the girls she had considered her closest friends would no longer talk to her. "I have been ready for the backstabbing my whole life," she lamented to *The Guardian*. "I lost a lot of people who I thought were my friends. Even the person who I thought was my best friend stopped speaking to me."

However, this type of experience wasn't new to her. "Growing up, I would experience jealousy from other girls because of my looks," she continued. "They had no need to be jealous, because they were beautiful themselves, but girls do have insecurities."

Yet, secretly, Rihanna had concerns about her own body, similar to those her bullies had harboured. "I'll never be perfect and there are things that bother me about myself, like my breasts," she added. "I wish I had bigger boobs. Every girl looks in the mirror and sees something they want to be different."

Whether her classmates had indeed been seething with jealousy or not, their abandonment came as a painful disappointment and a shock for Rihanna, who had wanted a 'true friend' to share her successes with. However, being alone only made her more determined, and she performed solo again in another musical talent show called Colours of Combermere.

Understandably, her previous partners in rhythm were devastated. "Kelenna is absolutely gorgeous," a former friend of both girls told the author, "but this was too much for her. Can you imagine the girl you thought was your friend getting a record producer while you get left out in the cold and then for her to have success in these shows? It really rubbed salt in her wounds when Rihanna sang at that pageant, because it was like saying not only could she sing better than her, but she was prettier than her too. To top that, Rihanna then stole her boyfriend. What did she have left?"

Rihanna's friend was referring to rumours that Rihanna had betrayed Kelenna, after they had tried to patch up their stormy friendship, by having sex with the man Kelenna was in love with. "It was insensitive," her friend continued. "She was singing the same song [at the pageant] that they sang together at lunchtimes at school, the one they'd entered the audition with, and the one that would make Rihanna famous. She knew she was headed for something good, so Kelenna felt like: couldn't she have been a bit more discreet? After all, it was Kelenna who'd lined up the audition to start with. It was her mother. Then she did this to her."

It had been a difficult end to the pair's friendship, with pain and anger on both sides. Meanwhile, the rumour mill was grinding overtime that Rihanna was renowned for sleeping with other girls' boyfriends.

However, by the time Rihanna turned 16 in February 2004, things had changed dramatically for her. Gone were the bullying girls and the pressures of school: she had been offered an escape route out of the island. With the Christmas demos half complete, Evan asked her why she had to wait until the next school holidays to come back. "That's when I knew it was serious," she recalled.

Rihanna applied for permission to study on the road and, released from the burdens of a restrictive school environment, accepted an invitation from Evan to move to his home in Connecticut. It was here that they would complete her first official demo.

"When I left Barbados, I didn't look back," she told *Entertainment Weekly*. "I wanted to do what I had to do, even if it meant moving to America."

That was exactly what it would take – and, one cold autumn morning, she was collected from the airport by Evan's wife, Jackie, to start her new life. If Jackie had been uncomfortable or insecure that a beautiful young starlet-in-the-making was sharing a home with her and her husband, she didn't show it. In fact, she became a mother figure to Rihanna and one of her closest allies. "Jackie definitely took on a mothering role," Rihanna told *Giant* magazine. "She took care of me when I was there. She made sure I had my laundry done. She made sure I ate on time." For someone who had been her own mother growing up, the nurture was a refreshing change – and she began to call her new parent 'auntie'.

"It's very much a family atmosphere," Evan concurred. "We've always had that kind of relationship, as opposed to some slick dealmaker swooping in and controlling her. We've always made sure that, even as young as she is, she is completely involved in all of the business and decisions and all that."

Yet, while Evan was quick to point out that she hadn't been manipulated in any way, Rihanna had a slightly different story, hinting that perhaps she still hadn't had as much control as she might have liked or expected. She told *The Guardian*, "When I first started, I didn't know anything. I didn't really have a say."

It was an uncomfortable experience, since she had been brought up by her mother to take an active role, instead of a back seat, in her own life. "My mom raised me to be a child and know my place, but also to think like a woman," she claimed. "She never held back from me in terms of being too young to know certain things, so I am very mature for my age."

Perhaps Rihanna wasn't getting the credit she deserved for thinking for herself but, in spite of that, she felt her career was in safe hands. She was also enjoying her new life in Connecticut, although the weather provided a horrifying culture shock. If she had been stifled in Barbados, both by the hot sun and the oppressive peers who wanted to see her fail, North America would prove to be equally troublesome – but this time because she was bitterly cold.

"We don't have seasons in Barbados, every day is by the pool or on the beach, so she had nothing to prepare her for America," a friend told the author. "She would phone me shivering, saying she couldn't keep warm even in the house and that she missed the sun... She didn't even own a coat before she left, and then I'd hear from her saying she'd been buying lots of cute jackets!"

Yet even warmer seasons proved a problem. Another culture shock came with Rihanna's laidback attitude to modesty, which didn't mix well with life in urban east-coast America. In Barbados, she had often stripped naked while she was at home due to the heat – and in the US, the pool cleaner had caught her several times. "At first it was so embarrassing," she told *Bravo*. "I always forget when he comes. I'm so confused when I have a day off, I usually sleep until noon and when I wake up, I don't even know what day it is. But he's used to this view now. I even told [best friend, Melissa] to text me when he comes, 'Rihanna, get dressed, the pool boy is here!'"

Yet, when she remembered to stay clothed, Connecticut was very rewarding for her. Evan had started writing songs of various genres for her and the four-track demo that was produced was aimed at showing off Rihanna's versatility.

'Last Time' was a slick R&B tune that wouldn't have sounded out of place on a Craig David CD, while 'Pon De Replay' was a dancehall-inspired, Caribbean-flavoured track designed to make the most of her roots. The final two tracks were Mariah Carey's 'Hero' and a Whitney Houston track that every self-respecting music producer would have been familiar with, 'For The Love Of You'.

The demo was intended to prove that, far from just a one-trick pony, Rihanna was capable of tackling any type of song she put her mind to. Evan began to prepare the demos to present to key figures in the industry. By this point, he had officially signed her to his label and provided her with her own lawyers – but if she thought that would get her out of school, she was mistaken.

"My mom always said, 'You're not stopping school until you get signed,' and even when I got signed, she still made me go to school," she groaned to *Glamour*. But this time, she had a personal tutor.

Another shock was in store for her when she was asked to change her name. Evan was planning to market her on her exotic heritage but he felt that her first name, Robyn — chosen by her Irish father — was too commonplace for a girl set to introduce a brand-new culture to American audiences.

"Robyn is an unusual name in the Caribbean, but my producer said it was a very popular name in the United States," she told *The Chicago Tribune*. "So when I told him my middle name, he preferred that because it was more unique."

Having signed with Evan's management team already, her name was officially changed to Rihanna and her demos sent out to potential record labels. Rihanna's heart skipped a beat when she heard that Island Def Jam, fronted by rap star Jay-Z, had heard her music and wanted to meet her in person. "Def Jam was the first label to call back," she told *Interview* magazine. "We got other calls, but they were the most enthusiastic."

Now that her work had come to the attention of Jay-Z, she knew she was in business. "I mean, I was 16 — from Barbados!" she continued incredulously. "Like, you would never... the chances of ever meeting somebody famous or ever being signed, that was just a deadly combination. Like, I had to meet Jay-Z and audition for him at the same time!"

As thrilled as she was, it was also a nerve-wracking moment. No longer would she be singing to stuffed toys or into pillows, as she had spent much of her childhood doing. Instead, she was standing before one of the biggest names in hip-hop, someone she had only previously seen on television while she dreamed wistfully of her own stardom — and she had to perform.

"The only previous time I'd sung in public was at a school concert," she recalled, "so I was pretty scared. But I just pretended that being in Jay-Z's office with him and five record company executives was an everyday event for me. Jay-Z was sitting there in his denim shorts and polo shirt, waiting to be impressed."

Rihanna had come from a meagre background – a lower-middle class family living in a very average part of town – and much of her parents' spare money had been swallowed by her father's crack cocaine addiction. She never had the privilege of singing lessons or dancing classes to hone her talent. Yet Jay-Z had come from an impoverished background too, growing up in a tough part of inner-city New York. As it turned out, he wasn't looking for polished perfection, but new talent. That was exactly what he was hoping to find that day in Rihanna.

Yet she was also nervous and sleep deprived. "The night before, I couldn't sleep," she recalled to *Glamour*. "I was trying on a million different outfits and make-up. I remember starting to shake [when I first saw Jay-Z]. I thought he would be in a suit, sitting behind a desk with a cigar. But he was totally chilled, wearing sneakers and a T-shirt. Then I went into audition mode. I knew it was all or nothing. Right away, the Def Jam people said, 'You can't leave the building.' They closed the door."

She had no choice but to throw herself into singing, although she quietly wondered whether a mad dash for the doors after last-minute jitters was commonplace in Jay-Z's office, hence the unusual precaution.

It was then that she finally relaxed. The butterflies in her stomach eased. The cold sweat trickling down the back of her neck stopped. The private demeanour that Evan had described as "painfully shy" took a back seat, and she was ready to show Jay-Z what she had.

When she had finished, Jay-Z was so keen to sign her that he told her the only escape route if she declined was through the window of his multi-storey office block. "They locked me into the office until 3 a.m.," Rihanna told *The Observer*. "And Jay-Z said, 'There's only two ways out. Out the door after you sign this deal − or through this window.' And we were on the 29th floor. Very flattering."

Jay-Z later told *Rolling Stone* that rarely for an artist − especially for one so young − she had offered both talent and swagger in one package, whereas he only needed the presence of one to seal a deal. "I signed her in one day," he said. "It took me two minutes to see she was a star."

As for Rihanna, like any teenager she couldn't wait to sign on the dotted line and struggled to control her patience. While a room full of legal advisers and record company executives talked their way through every minor detail of the contract, the 16-year-old felt that time was wasting. The scene mirrored the video for Britney Spears's 'Hit Me Baby One More Time' − a bored schoolgirl willing time to move faster so that she can break out and make her debut singing performance in the gym.

"My lawyers kept talking," she recalled to *The Observer* with frustration, "while I was looking at the clock waiting to sign!"

But she didn't have to wait long before her wishes were granted. She was ecstatic – but then it began to dawn on her that the real hard work was about to begin. While Rihanna had raw talent, natural aptitude and abundant enthusiasm, she still needed professional training. She had been watching Aaliyah and Destiny's Child videos over and over again and copying the dance moves religiously but – as someone who had never taken a dance class before in her life – it wasn't enough. She was fast-tracked to success by Def Jam, who had her spending eight hours each day with a choreographer. On top of that, she had to complete an additional 15 hours per week of school work to comply with child-labour laws in the USA. Meanwhile she was rehearsing her work, recording material for her debut album, doing meet-and-greets and travelling whenever necessary.

In fact, while recording, Rihanna even found time to join Gwen Stefani's Harajuku Girls tour in Japan as a support act, as well as undertaking a few select dates with 50 Cent in Canada. It was a gruelling schedule, but a privilege almost unheard of for a singer without an album to her name as yet, so Rihanna could barely complain. The previous year, she had been an innocent schoolgirl, who had barely even left her homeland – now she was living several thousand miles away in a foreign country before she had so much as taken her school exams. It was exciting, but simultaneously draining. As the glitter of the illusion began to fade, she quickly realised that – as rewarding as it might be – working with some of the top names in music was anything but easy.

"I grew up so much this year," she told *Belgrade Net*. "I had no choice. To pursue my dream, I left my entire family in Barbados to move to the States. It was a little scary to have no friends or family and all of a sudden step into a recording studio."

She added, "[It] taught me the dedication and responsibility it takes to make this dream a reality. Waking up at 5 a.m. to start rehearsals, the training, the school work, interviews, video shoots, going all day – it always seemed glamorous, but it is real work. My love for music and singing will never change, but the rose-coloured glasses are no longer so rosy."

Confessing to the press that he was working her at "an unbelievable breakneck pace", Jay-Z ushered her straight into the studio within days of signing her to record her first album. It would take just three months.

One of the first songs recorded was the title track, 'Music Of The Sun'. Although Rihanna was new to the songwriting process, and willing for now to take a back seat to the advice of others, she also wanted to make her mark and represent who she was and where she was from. On 'Music Of The Sun', one of the few tracks that she co-wrote, she achieved just that.

The lyric – which celebrated dance music as a universal pleasure, something as loved by everyone as the summer sun – meant a lot to her because she had been criticised for being 'too white' at school, had been made to feel like an outsider and accused of not authentically belonging to her culture. For that reason, she had wanted a song that was all-embracing, a metaphorical musical 'club' that anyone could join. Plus, no matter where someone was – even on a rainy winter evening in New York – she hoped the song would instantly transport them to the Caribbean paradise she was proud to call home. It was her way of conveying the energy and atmosphere of her hometown through music, and of making a statement that she was here to promote Caribbean culture, without compromise.

Other songs might not necessarily have been so much to Rihanna's tastes. 'Willing To Wait' was another song that she co-wrote; but also on the writing team was June Deniece Williams, a songwriter and soul singer, whose move into gospel had won her a string of Grammy Awards in the Eighties and Nineties. Indeed, Williams had once sung an acapella version of her tune 'God Is Amazing' live at the Grammys. Whatever else she offered, Williams' work didn't exactly give Rihanna R&B street cred. Plus, for someone who was trying to find her identity as 'a bad-ass girl', Williams' contribution might even have seemed counter-productive.

'Willing To Wait' was about a girl who fends off her boyfriend's advances, wanting to get to know him before they take the next step and end up in bed together. It seemed to suggest that Rihanna was surrounded by protective mother-hen types, who probably meant every word in their bid to shelter her from the world of men, whom they perceived as being out for sex and consequently not always meaning what they said. It's a point underlined by another of the song's co-writers, Susaye Green – who had sung with Ray Charles and The Supremes, and written with Stevie Wonder (for Michael Jackson, no less) – who spoke of her protégés as "very beautiful young people who are under pressure at all times because of their beauty and because they're young girls".

She told *Story of the Stars*: "A lot of people out there take advantage and I have been in that situation myself, so I understood it well. It is a heavy load." Perhaps in a direct nod to Rihanna, she added, "The only way I get involved with a 16-year-old is if I know their mother has been understanding and supportive, and is there all the time. I encourage them to write, to be entrepreneurs, strong business people. [For a 16-year-old to get my attention] she has to be pretty darn good!"

Clearly Rihanna fitted the bill – and, what with Susaye, June Deniece and her adopted 'uncles' Evan and Carl on songwriting duties, it was little wonder that the song had taken a protective tone. Yet it already seemed to have Rihanna typecast as a chaste virgin dead-set on abstention, just as one of Evan's other artists, Christina Aguilera, had been in her early days – but that might not be such a good thing in the hypersexual world of hip-hop. Would Rihanna even be marketable to her target crowd with those values? Meanwhile June Deniece's influences might have been better suited to a gospel artist or a smooth soul singer.

Yet Rihanna wasn't particularly concerned about the effects a God-fearing gospel soprano might have had on her reputation. After all, June Deniece had racked up 14 Grammy nominations by this time, four of which she had won. It sounded like she knew how to hit on a winning formula when it came to writing tunes.

Plus the song 'Let Me' was more Rihanna's style as, little by little, she came out of her shell. The chorus was teasingly ambiguous, suggesting either a sexually provocative invitation or the domestic pleasure of a demure housewife, eager to please the man she had innocently fallen in love with. Was it a lewd suggestion brought on by lust or something totally free from sexual connotations? The truth became apparent when things started hotting up in the verses, as Rihanna confessed that she might not be able to control herself if she got her man alone and let slip her penchant for seven-inch heels in the bedroom. Going from point-blank refusal of sex to a liberated account of her desire for a man, the CD seemed to be an eclectic mix already.

'Let Me' might have made Jackie, Evan's wife, wince, since it promoted Rihanna as a sexual being, as a bombshell who could well have been moving in on her territory and tempting her husband. However, the relationship was purely professional and Rihanna retained the support of the woman she described as her "second mother" – Jackie would even come to the studio from time to time to check on her.

While Rihanna didn't personally have a say in writing 'Let Me', she did have the input of Stargate, an up-and-coming Norwegian production duo who would break through in the US the following year with both her label-mate Ne-Yo's US and UK number one, 'So Sick', and 'Irreplaceable', a best-selling collaboration with Rihanna's ultimate idol, Beyoncé. Unusually, despite having associations with European pop artists such as S-Club 7, Billie Piper, Hear'Say, Blue, Samantha Mumba and Atomic Kitten, they still had some R&B street cred.

They had also gained rave reviews in *The New York Times*, which described their music as "sugary, lilting R&B in the Michael Jackson vein, leavened with the kind of melody-rich European pop that paints everything in bright primary colours… their work carries on a tradition of Scandinavian bubblegum artistry that stretched from Abba to [fellow producer] Max Martin."

Rihanna had never even heard of Abba. But for someone who wanted to shake up the reggae boundaries by blending Caribbean rhythms with the vibes of the New York or Los Angeles streets, or the urban sounds of a city such as London, Stargate might prove the ideal writing partners.

Kardinal Offishall, a Canadian-born rapper of Jamaican descent, who had performed on stage for the likes of Nelson Mandela, would also appear on the album. Known as 'Canada's hip-hop ambassador' to the in-crowd, he was known for blending traditional dancehall sounds with a modern R&B twist to appeal to worldwide audiences, no matter what their original musical tastes. That was exactly what Rihanna wanted to do and she was delighted to feature him on 'Rush'.

The track presents itself as a dialogue between a man and a woman who can't agree whether their romance is a love story or merely a lust story. In the song, Rihanna is infatuated, but for Offishall it is all about lust. The set-up echoed Jamaican dance-hall star Sean Paul's 'I'm Still In Love With You', a hit from the previous year, in which a woman can't bear to break their bond but the man can't handle the commitment, criticising her for falling too deeply in love and not seeing their fling for what it really is. For Paul's singing partner Sasha it is heartbreaking, but for Sean Paul it's merely harmless fun and he walks away from her. Sadly, on 'Rush', Rihanna falls prey to the same fate.

Meanwhile, on 'There's A Thug In My Life', Rihanna explores a similar, and typically Caribbean, theme. The track tells of a clandestine love affair with a man she knows her friends would never approve of, let alone her parents – someone she meets in secret after dark who she knows to be bad, but who treats her well. The age-old problem is conveyed when she asks how she will tell her mother that there's a thug at the centre of her life. Despite her elation, the assertion that the two will be together forever suggests uneasily that it's a story that can never end well. The thug in this case was voiced by rap artist J-Status, who featured on the track and was later also signed to SRP.

Continuing on the love theme, 'Now I Know' was another track co-written by Rihanna and it features an affair that turns to love quicker than either party can control it. She imagines the end of their relationship, agonising over the thought that love can change so suddenly and might pass as quickly as it had come.

'The Last Time' is excellent proof of that complaint. Rihanna might have been hurt, but she won't open her heart to get burned again – it's time for her to take power back into her own hands. The lyrics exorcise the end of a deceitful relationship, hitting home the message that she is calling the shots now – and she won't be coming back. 'That La La La', on the other hand, is a more upbeat number, with Rihanna telling a *faux* friend to back off and stop chasing after her man, because their love can never be broken by an outsider. This song was scorned in Barbados and, as a friend of hers recalls, saw those who bought into the rumours of Rihanna being promiscuous dub her an "unforgivable hypocrite".

Yet Rihanna was unrepentant and refused to listen to her detractor's "unfounded lies".

Her pride was partially restored by the presence of two strong producers on the track. Full Force, a six-strong group of hip-hop singers, songwriters and producers were a big name in the industry already, having worked with the Backstreet Boys on 'All I Have To Give', Prince's ex-wife Mayte on *Child Of The Sun* – which was regrettably left unreleased – and the ultimate tough girl of hip-hop, L'il Kim, on her song 'Can't Fuck With Queen Bee'. They were also renowned for writing and producing almost every hit single on *La Toya*, the fifth album from La Toya Jackson, and had also worked with Bob Dylan, The Black Eyed Peas and Britney Spears – an eclectic mix of artists.

D'Mile, on the other hand, was almost unknown when he turned his attention to the track, but its success would later propel him to fame, earning him contracts with Mary J. Blige, Justin Bieber and Janet Jackson.

'Here I Go Again' was a more simple affair – a writing collaboration between Rihanna, her two newfound uncles and J-Status. The song speaks of an time-honoured predicament around the world: addictive love. Months or perhaps even years after a relationship has gasped its final breath, Rihanna realises she hasn't entirely closed the door on her feelings – and, regardless of who she has dated since, she can't forget the one love she lost. J-Status's role is to encourage the indecisive ex to set the fire burning again.

Another collaboration took place on the legendary reggae/soul heartbreak song 'You Don't Love Me (No, No, No)', originally performed by its writer, Dawn Penn. It was an ambitious cover version and Jamaican dancehall artist Vybz Kartel was brought in to provide additional vocals.

There was speculation at the time whether Rihanna could live up to Dawn's definitive rendition and, in particular, whether she could pull off the deep-soul singing of a much older woman, with years of heartbreak already behind her. But it was immediately obvious to those in the studio that Rihanna had conquered the song by 'making it her own'.

Bonus tracks on the album included 'Hypnotised', a special extra on the Japanese edition, and 'Should I', another collaboration with J-Status.

However, the heart of the album was in songs like 'If It's Loving That You Want'. According to Evan, it was the prospect of tracks like this – a lazy, gentle reggae rhythm melded with a sultry voice delivered in an exotic Bajan lilt – that had led him to sign her "without hesitation". She had cross-cultural appeal, both in her look and her sound. She could represent white, black and mixed-race girls all at once – and, of course, she could represent Barbados.

Meanwhile, the track benefited from a sample of 'The Bridge Is Over' by Boogie Down Productions. The lyrics promised fantastic love from a lady who was beautiful, caring and mesmerising, while the groove promised an authentic delivery of music from the land of the sun. For Evan, it was an irresistible combination – but that was nothing compared to the track 'Pon De Replay', one of the songs from her demo.

Rihanna had been reluctant to record the song to begin with, feeling it was a dumbed-down, children's pop version of the reggae classics she had been accustomed to back home. She worried that it would end up a no-man's land between a lifeless pop number and a contrived dancehall effort. "When I first heard that song, I didn't want to do it because it was very sing-songy and very – whatever. Nursery rhymish," she told *Artist Direct*. However, she didn't let her inhibitions get the better of her. She was so eager to succeed that she swallowed her reservations and wholeheartedly gave herself up to being a star. The effort was worthwhile.

"After I started recording it, I went along with it and started liking it – and people loved it!" In fact, Evan loved it so much that he made it her first single.

"We agreed that there were several songs which could be the first single," she explained to *Singer Universe*, "but 'Pon De Replay' was selected because it seemed like the song that would be best suited for a summer release." Eager to prove it, their next step would be to create an accompanying promo video. Rihanna wanted her first release to be perfect, so she teamed up with veteran choreographer Fatima Robinson to bring her dance moves up to date.

Fatima's credits included working with The Black Eyed Peas ('My Humps') and Fergie on her sexy, street-style video, 'London Bridge' – so Rihanna knew she was in safe hands.

The director chosen also had good pedigree. Little X had been in the game since the 1990s, notably producing the video for Sean Paul's first hit, 'Gimme the Light', which helped propel the self-declared "dancehall legend" to stardom. Little X had also directed Kanye West's 'The New Workout Plan', Eve and Alicia Keys' 'Gangsta Lovin'', Usher's 'You Got It Bad', Christina Aguilera's 'Tilt Your Head Back' and Alicia Keys' 'You Don't Call Me'.

Like all of these numbers, 'Pon De Replay' featured a simple video. The party starts off low-key until Rihanna makes her entrance, changes the vibe and commands the DJ to turn the music up so she can dance, looking angelic while gyrating to the music in a crop top and tight blue jeans.

That demand would set the scene for the rest of her career. Radio shows all over the country duly obeyed and, following its August 22, 2005 release, 'Pon De Replay' flooded the charts. The beat was catchy and it didn't hurt that the public thought Rihanna was looking as sizzling as the late summer sun that the track was timed to coincide with.

However, for some newcomers to its Caribbean heart, it needed a translation. "It's just language that we speak in Barbados," Rihanna chuckled to *Kidz World* by way of explanation. "It's broken English. 'Pon' is on, 'De' means the, so it's just basically telling the DJ to put my song on the replay."

All Rihanna could now do was sit and wait – but she didn't have to wait for long. "I was in a shopping centre when I heard it for the first time on the radio," she recalled. "I was jumping up and down screaming, 'That's my song!', and everyone was looking at me like I was completely nuts, naturally enough! It was a strange time for me, because everyone was telling me I was the new Beyoncé. I was just 17 and having private tuition to make up for not being at school."

Despite the elation, she remained nervous about her place in the music industry. The week Rihanna's single was released in the UK, for example, she was up against the decade-old Britpop battle between Oasis and Blur – the latter in the form of Gorillaz, led by ex-Blur front man Damon Albarn. She sounded totally different from anything else in the charts at the time – was the Western world prepared for her interpretation of lazy, late-summer reggae?

Meanwhile, although Rihanna definitely had sex appeal in her deck of cards, could she match the full-on, all-out sexuality of a group like The Pussycat Dolls, who were now flavour of the month both in the UK and stateside, with 'Don't Cha'? She could play the R&B card too, but was she edgy enough for that audience, given that tracks like 'Willing To Wait' seemed to shadow the Christina Aguilera of 'Genie In A Bottle', suggesting a brand of teenage innocence normally not given the time of day in that genre? Her team might have been marketing her as an exotic addition to the charts, but she was fretting that it might not work in her favour – plus, even if it did, did she want to be a novelty act marketed purely on hailing from everyone's favourite holiday destination? Perhaps she wanted to mix up the beats instead.

She also had to compete with a trend for indie ballads, such as Coldplay's 'Fix You' and David Gray's 'The One That I Love', as well as electro-dance club classics such as Mylo's 'Dr Pressure'. There was so much to contend with. Plus the tantalising prospect of knocking her biggest idol – and now rival – Mariah Carey, off her throne in the USA made her head spin. It was a thought she barely dared to contemplate. Even more terrifyingly, despite the positive reassurances of her team, would she even make the charts at all?

Her prayers were answered when she quickly earned a number two spot in America, just behind Mariah Carey's 'We Belong Together'. By October, the song would go on to knock Axel F's novelty ringtone track 'Crazy Frog' off the number one spot. She also peaked at number two in the UK, losing out to Oasis by a whisker for the top spot, number six in Australia and number seven in Canada.

Suddenly, everywhere that Rihanna went, people were humming her tune and, less than a week after the song's release, she was invited to perform at the pre-show for the 2005 MTV Video Music Awards on August 28. It was a defining moment for her and it allowed her to put Barbados on the map.

"It is such an honour to carry the torch for Barbados and the rest of the Caribbean," she told *The Guardian* later. "When I performed at the Video Music Awards, so many people had the Barbados flag, and people back home saw that and were just so touched. They had never seen a Bajan artist on the international stage like that before, which is amazing. Sometimes, when you have that kind of support, you feel like you could take on the world."

Of course, the world was next on her list – but not before the release of her first album, *Music Of The Sun*, on August 30. Rihanna would be up against the rock, pop and dancehall fusion anthems of Gwen Stefani, who had flirted with westernising trademark reggae sounds for some time; the exotic, fellow mixed-race singer Amerie, whose hit 'One Thing' had smashed the charts earlier in the year; the South American sensation Ciara, who had the support of Missy Elliott for her own chart hit, 'Oh'; the buxom burlesque soundtracks of The Pussycat Dolls; the light-hearted white rapper Lady Sovereign; and the counter-cultural Sri Lankan dissident M.I.A, who never failed to add a bit of tongue-in-cheek politics to the mix.

But this was Rihanna's time, too. She played a couple of shows to promote the release, including the USA Lawn Tennis Championships Open on August 29 and subsequently the NFL Championships kick-off on September 8.

It was now down to the bloggers and reviewers to offer their thoughts – and Jay-Z was predicting mayhem. He warned, "The biggest advice I can give to her is to keep her circle tight because she can't control anything else outside of that. She can't control people's opinions of her records or what's being said on the blogs… but if she has the proper friends, she won't get caught up in the wild-child lifestyle."

He also advised her not to get accustomed to the fame, or become too big-headed, because it could all be taken away in a moment. "He said, 'You must be a good person, because good things are happening for you, but you have to stay humble,'" Rihanna recalled to *Glamour*. "One thing that intrigued me about him was that he was such a huge artist and really down to earth. I felt like if he was saying this, it must work."

Indeed, Rihanna would have to remain down to earth to survive the deluge of press – both positive and negative – following the album release. The rumour mill glowed red with one controversial claim – that some of Kardinal Offishall's lyrics for 'Rush' were demeaning to her, suggesting that she had slept her way into showbiz or, at the very least, that it was her sex appeal and the promise of titillation that had made fame possible. Specifically, whether it was on the dancefloor or in the bedroom, the lyrics seemed to say that ass-shaking had created her career. Of course, the girls who gloated that Rihanna had slept with Jay-Z to earn her place in the industry were rubbing their hands together with glee at this latest piece of gossip, probably sparing little thought for Rihanna's agony.

To make matters worse, *Pop Matters* reviewed the album by saying, "I noticed that there's some heavy hitters batting behind this marginally talented young singer... Kardinal Offishall [for example]."

It wasn't just the innuendoes that hurt, but the wounding slight that it was her collaborators who were holding the songs together, compensating for a somehow weak or patchy vocal from her side. The review continued mockingly, "From her baggy jeans to her adequate Caribbean-inflected vocals, it all seemed so perfect (maybe a little too perfect)... the 'Pon De Replay' video should be held up as the prototype for shrewd star making."

The implication was clear: that she was heavily manufactured by a team of song writers to mask a lack of genuine talent and that her success was down to her connections, good fortune and physical assets. Still, Jay-Z had warned the criticism wouldn't be easy to swallow – and he had years of experience fending it off.

It wasn't the only bad word she would have to read about herself, either. *Epinions* insisted that the album was "stale" and that tracks like 'Rush' were "pure filler". *Entertainment Weekly* reported that the album was "filled with maudlin arrangements that block out the music of the sun".

Not everyone liked her hit single 'Pon De Replay' either. An ex-classmate told the author, "There was something a bit patronising about it, like the style was being toned down to suit white ears. It ended up a no-man's land between dancehall and pop, so it just ended up sounding lame."

The highly respected *Rolling Stone*, on the other hand, had awarded top marks to the track, crediting it as a "poppy piece of dancehall reggae, with slapping, syncopated beats recalling big-band jazz". Yet her ex-classmate's comments echoed Rihanna's original concerns about the track, when she had fretted, "I didn't like 'Pon De Replay' at first.

I thought it sounded like a nursery rhyme. It didn't sound like singing. It wasn't music that I was used to."

Could the problem be that producers Evan and Carl, despite being hugely successful with the careers of candy-coated boy bands, were total novices at producing successful tracks on the reggae scene? People speculated that they had chosen to dabble in the genre to honour their Bajan wives without truly knowing enough about it. They were out of the territory of slushy love songs now – Rihanna was nothing like *NSYNC or Christina Aguilera – and they had plunged into the deep end with their first dancehall-inspired track. However, no matter what the critics said, the CD sales spoke for themselves. After just 27 weeks in the charts, the song had gone platinum, marking over a million copies sold. Whatever the results of their experiment, there was no denying that it had been popular.

What might have been of more concern to Rihanna was the complaint, doled out by *The Boston Herald*, that "her range is non-existent and the lyrics might seem a bit childish to the post-pubescent crowd".

"The one thing Rihanna didn't want to be was childish," a friend says. "She was worried about the responsibility of all the kids looking up to her. She also wanted respect in the industry. She wasn't 100% sure what she wanted to be, but she did know for sure that a kid's entertainer wasn't it."

Indeed, it might have been good for her popularity to market her to the young, but Rihanna might also have felt a tinge of unfulfilment, a sneaking suspicion that she was being untrue to herself. She was growing up fast and, while being touted as a wholesome influence for young teens with an emphasis on sexual restraint and chastity might have been adequate for now, what would happen when she wanted to express a more adult side of her personality later?

Common Sense Media, a website advising on the suitability of media and merchandise for children, gave Rihanna the tick of approval, stating, "The music is infectious, the lyrics are clever, the performances and production sparkle... Rihanna, still a teenager herself, delivers music as warm and bright as a Caribbean sunrise." It was good that her songs could be perceived as child-friendly, but was it all a little too nice?

Perhaps. But while she was still unsure what she wanted to be, she was for the time being happy to hand the reins over to her team of professionals.

Fortunately for her, although some of the reviews were negative, others were blissfully complimentary. According to *The Daily Telegraph*, "she already has a tick in every female R&B box, thanks to her arresting voice, cover-girl looks and a beach rags-to-riches story." The review added, "A confident cover of 'You Don't Love Me (No, No, No)' saves her from airbrushed anonymity, while the slang request for DJs to play her single 'on the replay' looks set to be a wish granted the world over." If only all requests could be so simple.

Amazon lauded her as a "fresh new female face of reggae" – a delight to Rihanna, who had always complained that the scene both internationally and back home was dominated by male artists, not giving women a look in. It looked like a wrong she stood a realistic chance of putting right.

Sputnik, meanwhile, countered previous complaints that Rihanna was supported almost entirely by the skill of guest vocalists and unseen song writers by highlighting that, "The skills of Sturken-Rogers and vocal nuance of Rihanna go hand in hand to make songs that can be thoroughly enjoyed."

Finally, *Star Pulse* was also won round, declaring, "Initially it was tempting to discount Rihanna as yet another Beyoncé-Ciara-Ashanti cash-in... But Rihanna is winsome rather than wannabe... one of the more engaging urban dance pop albums of the year."

When Rihanna had first entered the business, she had suffered delusions of 'glam'deur, but she had soon realised that the fashionable, exciting new life she had always craved didn't live up to her glamorous expectations – and was a lot more hard work than it seemed. However, when she read the glowing reviews, it made her insanely heavy workload all seem worthwhile.

Chapter 3

Back in the Land of the All-Day Sun

As Rihanna prepared to hit the streets for her first major tour, to be sponsored by Secret Body Spray, a wave of fan mail hit her Myspace account. Rihanna's name was the new buzzword on every R&B blog while her single was climbing DJs' playlists fast. Hysterical fans poured out internet love letters. Girls wanted to be her and boys wanted to be with her. While some wrote declarations of love, clamouring to know whether she had a boyfriend, others exclaimed with equal passion, "I wish she could be my sister!" Fortunately, Rihanna was willing to work the crowds and was lapping up all the attention.

"I was at an ice cream shop one day and there was this flock of children, maybe 16 of them, and they all started grabbing napkins and they were like 'Can I have an autograph, please?'" she recalled excitedly to MTV. "That was a moment for me because I used to be in that position. I would see a star, just beg for their autograph. And then for people to be asking me, I felt honoured!"

It was a dream come true. However, not everyone's intentions were quite so innocent and Rihanna again found herself fending off rumours that she had slept her way to the top. She was discovering all too quickly the price of fame.

One of Rihanna's school classmates told *Media Takeout,* "I believe to this day that she forced herself on Jay-Z because she is extremely promiscuous… old habits never die."

Rihanna was prepared for – albeit disgusted by – these revelations. "It was like, 'Of course she had to give Jay-Z a blowjob to get that deal.' That rumour was everywhere… and it was so disgusting. It made me feel really weird – I would even be weird around Jay-Z," she recalled.

Meanwhile, if she had hoped Barbados would be a safe haven away from the criticism of mainstream America, she was to be sorely mistaken. If anything, the opposition was worse. "It's a silly way of Barbadians," she told *The Observer.* "They always have to find fault, they're waiting for you to fall. As much as they enjoy your success and are like, 'Keep it up,' they have so much pride, it's easier for them to say, 'Little whore, you slept with Jay-Z to get signed.' Even when I go back there now, I'll see girls in the street, walking and snubbing and saying stuff about me."

Some girls she had known all of her life blanked her completely, while others simply gave her 'death stares'. Rumours circulated that she had been so hapless at school – and so intent on partying – that she had had to repeat the entire eight and ninth grades. Her proud father Ronald was forced to retort that, in fact, she had been one of the brightest girls in the school.

Yet most embarrassing of all for her were the accusations of X-rated action with her mentor. She struggled to look Jay-Z in the eye until, guessing what was wrong, he offered her some advice from seasoned experience.

"One day he called," she told *The Observer,* "and he was like, 'Yo, you can't buy into these rumours, you can't let people move you with anything they say.' The rumours started getting very funny to me after that."

That was just as well, as the stories on the street were becoming increasingly outlandish. One read that Beyoncé, then Jay-Z's fiancée, had pushed Rihanna downstairs in a fit of jealous rage, breaking her wrist in the process. Even worse, Rihanna felt obliged to read every last one.

"I wouldn't know what was being said, and then I'd get asked about [the rumours] and I'm like, '*What?*'" Rihanna joked. "I have to know what's being said about me, so I know what to expect. So me and my friends will go on an internet gossip site and look this stuff up. But it's kind of sick how people read it and think this is their way to knowledge, that they know all about you."

However, when she made it out on tour, the stress all became worthwhile. For her, nothing could beat the thrill of thousands of fans screaming her name. One stand-out show was her first charity concert, at City Place Mall, in Washington's Silver Spring. The show, on November 8, 2005, was a fundraiser hosted by local radio station Hot 99.5 for the victims of the recent Hurricane Katrina. Rihanna had promised the station a free performance if it sold all of its fundraising bracelets. While a cheque for £6,000 was presented to Hot 99.5, Rihanna appeared, to the sound of her new fans' hysterical screams.

She was flanked by a police escort, sheltering her from an adoring, if over-enthusiastic, crowd. Bloggers spoke of "excessive screaming" and fights breaking out as to which audience members had discovered her first or were "her biggest fans". For a girl who had been anonymous a few short months before, it was awe-inspiring.

The show started with the Dawn Penn cover from her album, 'You Don't Love Me (No, No, No)' and ended with a medley of choruses from artists across the board, including Kanye West and Sean Paul. A sea of camera phones appeared overhead, not retreating until the last verse of the final song. What was more, according to *Silver Chips Online*, "her voice could hardly be heard over the boisterous bass of the background music and the teenage boys confessing their love to her." Finally, Rihanna made her rock'n'roll exit, ushered away by another police escort and disappearing out of sight as quickly as she had arrived.

The live shows were an opportunity for Rihanna to build an identity of her own and shake off the endless references to her in the media as a "poor man's Beyoncé". According to the press, the similarities weren't just in looks either. *The Daily Telegraph* reported that 'Let Me' was a "dead ringer for Beyoncé's 'Naughty Girl'", while *Slant* magazine called

'Pon De Replay' "a dancehall-pop mixture that owes plenty of its sweat and shimmy to Beyoncé's 'Baby Boy'."

Perhaps the comparisons were inevitable, thanks to the Jay-Z connection, but to Rihanna – who desperately wanted to be recognised as a singer in her own right – the comments were wearing thin.

The rumours of a feud between the two women were also reaching their peak. However, Rihanna was at least able to put those to rest with an account of the first time she met her idol. "I did an industry performance and Beyoncé came," Rihanna told *InStyle*. "I froze. I whispered, 'You're my idol, thanks for coming!' and she said, 'Aww, you're so sweet!'" It wasn't quite the catfight that the media had been hoping for.

Plus, for anyone in any further doubt, Rihanna had publicised her infatuation the previous month with a public performance of a tribute to the now disbanded Destiny's Child. By her side were pop sensations Amerie and Teairra Mari, both of whom had been signed that year – the latter also by Jay-Z. Together, the trio had performed a rendition of 'Lose My Breath' at the MTV World Music Awards on September 13. This was the song that Rihanna had been replaying endlessly prior to getting signed so she could memorise all of the hip-hop dance moves. Little could she have imagined that, months later, she would be performing it on stage for real. It turned out the dance moves she'd made for fun had just been an audition. And, as she had been keen to point out, there was definitely no bad blood between her and Beyoncé. "She was a very big influence to me since I was a little girl," she confirmed to *Digital Spy*.

Meanwhile, rather than feuding, she had been working hard, paying her dues and performing to anyone who wanted to see her. That had even meant doing shows at unfashionable venues such as Toys 'R' Us, but she hadn't been deterred. Even if it was a threat to her credibility as a serious artist, she was willing to play anywhere if it would help her hit the big time.

"Rihanna is a hard worker," producer Evan Rogers confirmed. "She loves what she does, so she makes our job easier. It is extremely difficult to break into the United States market, but Rihanna has – and her future looks very bright."

She set out to prove his point by adding the filming of a promotional video for the single 'If It's Loving That You Want' to her hectic schedule. The promo was a chance for Rihanna to get back to her roots, as it was filmed on a stretch of utopian Californian coastline that matched the scenery back home. The plot was generic, featuring a bronzed, fresh-faced and photogenic young Rihanna seducing the camera by rolling provocatively on the sandy beach, as well as dancing on the shore.

"This video is about having fun, giving off the vibe of the Caribbean," Rihanna told MTV on the set of the shoot. "We did some mermaid-looking stuff down on the sand and I'm just performing to the camera as if it were my boyfriend... it's going to be incredible." Indeed, cavorting in front of the cameras had already become almost second nature. She added, "The song is basically telling a guy, 'If it's loving that you want, you should make *me* your girl, because I've got what you need!'"

The shoot also offered an opportunity for fun. Besides belly-dancing, there were jet-ski scenes – something Rihanna had to be taught how to ride. Despite hailing from a town by the Caribbean sea, she had never ridden one before. As someone from a low-income family, such luxuries had never been accessible to her. The gap between her modest background growing up and the life of undeniable glitz and glamour she was entering was beginning to become apparent.

She seemed determined to make up for lost time, in fact. As she added to MTV, "The water was so cold, but oh my gosh, we had so much fun! We were bumping each other off the jet skis and just had a ball!"

The pressure was back on by November 3, however, when she was nominated for her first award at the MTV Europe Music Awards in Lisbon. She competed alongside Kaiser Chiefs, James Blunt, Daniel Powter and Akon for the title of Best New Act. On November 21, she performed for the launch of a brand new Caribbean music channel on MTV Networks and, shortly afterwards, hooked up with the Jamaican-based Elephant Man to do an official remix for 'Pon De Replay'. "We used him because it's such an energetic song and we needed a hype, man!" Rihanna told MTV. "And Elephant Man? He's the energy king!"

Her commitments were coming hard and fast now, sometimes requiring her to visit more than one city per day. Yet hard work was finally beginning to reap rewards when Rihanna was allowed the luxury of a private jet to fly her to and from engagements. She was finally living the dream.

November also saw the official release of 'If It's Loving That You Want', which earned a modest but respectable chart position, peaking at number 36 in the USA and number 11 in the UK, and achieving Top 10 places in Australia, New Zealand and her father's ancestral homeland, Ireland.

At around the same time, the news broke that she had been nominated in no fewer than 10 categories for the first ever annual Barbados Music Awards. Following that, Rihanna also bagged a sponsorship to promote the island to tourists from around the world with a series of 30-second TV adverts. "I was so thrilled to be able to play a small part in the promotion of Barbados – the country I grew up in and the country which made me who I am," she enthused to *Groove* magazine. "I will attempt to continue to use my creative efforts to highlight Barbados, so everyone will know what a wonderful country it is!"

She was overjoyed, but the excitement was bittersweet for Rihanna. Behind the scenes, a public backlash had begun, pioneered by those who disapproved of what she did and how they felt it reflected on the island. In fact, things became so volatile that the country's culture minister, Stephen Lashley, even publicly spoke out in support of her, branding Rihanna a home-grown talent and urging followers to court, not criticise her.

Rihanna hadn't expected the criticism. Whether it was jealousy, conservative beliefs or personal dislike that she was contending with, she had stirred up controversy by her mere presence. On January 9, 2006 she jetted back into her hometown for the awards ceremony at Bridgetown's Sherbourne Centre. Joining her was her ex-drill sergeant from her days in cadets, Shontelle Layne. Her presence wasn't a surprise to Rihanna, as she had spotted her in America already, and had learned for the first time of Shontelle's secret aspirations to top the charts. Shontelle told *US* magazine, "As much as we grew up together, neither one of us had any clue the other wanted to be a singer. I remember the first time we saw each other in New York and she had just gotten signed. We were just like, 'Oh my God, this is so crazy. I didn't know you wanted to be a singer!' She was like, 'Dude, I didn't know *you* wanted to be a singer!'"

Rihanna may have feared Shontelle's harsh punishments in cadets, but, as Shontelle often joked to her, she was "the big boss now", with her former sergeant boasting just two nominations to Rihanna's 10. Rihanna was overloaded with gongs on the night too, winning the categories for Best Reggae/Dancehall Album, Best Dance Single, Best New Artist, Best Selling Female Artist, Song of the Year, Female Artist of the Year, Album of the Year and finally Entertainer of the Year.

Some might have wondered, witnessing the receipt of so many trophies, whether she was the only vocalist in the country. Yet she was definitely the most famous one. By that time, *Music Of The Sun* had hit the Top 10 on the US *Billboard* chart and would go on to sell two million copies worldwide – 69,000 in its first week of release alone.

It seemed that she was also among friends when it came to representing the country, as Shontelle won the category for Song Writer of the Year. If that had inspired a tinge of jealousy in Rihanna, who allowed most of her songs to be written for her, she didn't show it. Friendly rivalry was the flavour of the night.

Yet Rihanna's celebrations were soon marred by criticism. Even the dress she had worn to the ceremony became a topic for angry speculation. One fan raged on an internet forum, "Rihanna has beauty and talent. She does not need to wear a dress like the one she wore on the night to gain fame. Do you think if she had turned up elegantly dressed and not so exposed that she would have been less popular?"

That question hung in the air as Rihanna publicly thanked the residents of Barbados for "really supporting me". Underneath the smile for the cameras, she was seething at the reception she had been given by her fellow Bajans. She accused them of hypocrisy, using her as a tool for promotion, but simultaneously criticising her every chance they got. In turn, some Barbadians branded Rihanna a hypocrite, too, because she spoke publicly of her adoration for her country and its people, but behind closed doors was far less shy about criticising them to the international press.

"They talk shit about me all the time," she had snapped to *Entertainment Weekly*. "But I'm like, 'Whatever. I'm still doing this because I love to do it and you're not going to stop me.'" She added, "It really annoys me when [it's] people that I try to represent and I try to put them on the map as much I can. You know, I didn't have to put tridents [the symbol of the Barbadian flag] in my videos. I didn't have to talk about them. I didn't have to even mention that I'm from Barbados. But I do and people kind of take it for granted."

Meanwhile, to others she gushed about the honour of carrying the torch for Barbados, telling one of the island's national newspapers, *Weekend Nation,* "I love Barbados and anything I can do to promote the country and say thanks to the island, I would be eager to do. Barbados has given me a foundation that I am grateful for."

The dark side of her two-headed love-hate relationship continued to emerge when she spoke to *The Guardian*. "In Barbados, we have this pride thing. People hate to give up compliments. It physically hurts them to say congratulations – they find it easier to be mean."

But all of the controversy had planted a seed of inspiration in Rihanna's head for material for the new album. She had returned to the studio to jam within a month of her debut album being released, trying to put together a new offering. And now, she was starting to record in earnest. "We just felt it was time," she said, explaining her unusual decision to move so fast to *Artist Direct*. "It made no sense waiting. You should never put time on music. You should never say, 'OK, *Music Of The Sun* has to be out for at least a year and a half before we start with… No. That's what's great about the music business, when you feel it's time, you just go for it… we pretty much dived right in."

Yet there were some tough sacrifices to be made. Sleepless nights, under-eye circles and a generous supply of concealer became regular parts of the furniture. "We were still promoting the first album, still promoting the first singles and we just had to fit [recording] in where we could, like at the end of the day. Like, at 11:30 at night, we would start… we had no time," Rihanna told *MP3*.

It wasn't just sleep and spare time that she had to sacrifice. She had been keen to promote 'Let Me' as a third single from *Music Of The Sun*, telling MTV, "It's a very flirty, very naughty song. I'm basically telling this guy, 'Let me do those things for you.' It's very sexy."

Unfortunately, due to the lack of time, the single never saw the light of day in the West. Instead, it became a Japanese-only release to titillate the new fans she had made supporting Gwen Stefani on her Harajuku Lovers tour the previous year.

While that single was shared among its limited audience, Rihanna was working on her first new track, 'S.O.S'. The song details an addictive love affair with a man she can't break away from, someone who dominates all of her waking thoughts. "It's all about being rescued from this crazy feeling that this guy gives me – so I call out for help," she told MTV. Behind Rihanna's plaintive vocal trapezing, as she begs for help and complains that she has lost her mind, is a carefully blended sample of UK electro-pop duo Soft Cell's 1982 classic, 'Tainted Love'.

Many people, both before and after, would tinker with the song – from burlesque sensation The Pussycat Dolls to the gothic-tinged Marilyn Manson and the ultra-camp Boy George – but, according to fans, no-one's interpretation was quite as unique as Rihanna's.

OMM would later describe the song as "outrageously hooky" while, according to *The Observer*, it was "a fine bid for world domination". Indeed, it seemed to onlookers that – despite her protestations of not being in control – Rihanna hoped to be exactly that, with the tune seeking a forceful grip on the charts. "We knew instantly it was single material," an anonymous mixer in the studio explained. "Christina Milian turned down the song, but Rihanna's team didn't need asking twice – to them, it was an instant hit."

Rihanna had to put her trust in the judgement of others because, although she had heard Soft Cell before, she had no idea whether the sample was commercially credible in the USA. And synthpop wasn't the only new style she was exploring and making her own. She didn't need much persuasion to experiment with rock music either.

"Growing up in Barbados, I wasn't exposed to a lot of rock music," she explained to MTV. "We really love reggae and soca music and hip-hop.

I was exposed to a lot of different types of music [when I arrived in the US], rock being one of them," she continued, "and I fell in love with it. Now I *love* rock music." Yet she wasn't about to betray her island roots either, enthusing, "I'm super inspired by reggae. It's been a part of me since I was born."

The solution was to create a track that blended the two – a combination of both rock and reggae – and that song was 'Kisses Don't Lie'. She'd received inspiration from watching Gwen Stefani's flirtation with the two genres on stage every night in Japan, but she wanted to produce something a little more forceful, à la Damien Marley's 'Welcome To Jamrock'. "I decided I wanted to be creative and put some rock and reggae together," she explained to MTV, "but the album is not overall a rock influence – just that one song."

Just as the sound fuses heavy electric guitars with an incongruent reggae beat, the lyrics portray two opposites as well. Tempted by the kisses of a lover, she is afraid to let her guard down until she knows that he's sincere. Her uncertainty over the fictional romance also reflected her feelings about men in real life. "Every time I meet someone now, I always keep my guard up," she told *Men's Fitness*. "It's like a reflex action. He hits on me and my guard is up. Like, I have to find every reason why he can't be the guy. I just drill him. I make guys go through hell sometimes. Some of these guys are just too slick, but I'm ready for them."

In the battle between her heart and her head in 'Kisses Don't Lie', it is unclear which will be victorious, but there is no such debate musically – both rock and reggae are there to stay. *Pop Matters* would later praise how representative it felt the song was of her, claiming, "I don't think it's a coincidence that she's credited with co-writing this tune – she sounds inspired."

Rihanna felt the same, telling *Artist Direct,* "Oh yeah, the music is much closer to my heart this time around. Much more personal. Everything speaks about what it's like to be a girl like me."

Sadly for Rihanna, 'Dem Haters' fitted that description too. A song about *faux* friends with jealous hearts, its upbeat reggae rhythm carries a vocal warning about those who bitterly envied her success. It was exactly how she felt about her reception back home.

The tourist board had showered her with praise, with executive Bill Silvermintz gushing, "Rihanna is truly an outstanding Barbadian and someone who should be praised for her love of the country and her intelligence. She has become a spokesperson for Barbados and she is not asking for one penny."

Yet his warmth was countered by the many others who seemed to hate Rihanna's guts. The very people she had expected to congratulate her were still shunning her. Some claimed she had transformed into a pop tart, selling her soul – and possibly her body – to make it in the music world. Some appeared to scorn her, accusing her of promiscuity and alleging she had slept with their friends' boyfriends. For others, her clothing was too revealing for their strict moral code. It was even suggested that Rihanna was not a true Bajan girl because her skin was too pale.

And there was another, darker debate at hand too. Some Barbadians objected to the apparent influence of calypso and soca rhythms on Rihanna's music. The songs might have sounded upbeat, but – back in the days of colonial slavery – their writers were anything but.

Paul Browne, who attended the same church and school as Rihanna, explains: "Calypso was developed under slavery and it was a way to get back at the white owners with irreverent songs and dances, often mocking the whites. This they in turn allowed."

In fact, calypso's dark history is rooted in the slaves' reaction to French customs such as carnival, which were exported to the French colonies. Slaves could only watch wistfully as the colourful, glamorous celebrations went on around them until, one day, in a vengeful moment of defiance, they decided to make their own music. However, while people such as plantation owners might have turned a blind eye, the church apparently did not.

Paul continues: "The church then, as it is now, was never keen on the 'natives getting restless' and urged obedience to masters and respect for authority. Even though the islands have all attained political self-determination, the church and big business are still conservative and continues to feel that this form of self-expression is unhelpful."

It was a disapproval shared by some of Rihanna's 'haters' as well. Some felt the rhythms symbolised slavery, a tragic past that they shouldn't be tied to and would rather forget. But others countered that, even with chains on, victims had risen above their enslavement and that their resilience ought to be celebrated, instead of buried. They were offended at the suggestion that such a significant part of their history could be erased. Yet in spite of what these Barbadians criticised as 'censorship' of their culture, others remained devoutly religious and loyal to the church.

A number of the latter were simply not happy with Rihanna – and they found it even more offensive that a girl who was 'half white' could be 'mocking' them by turning to calypso culture. "That's absolutely preposterous," says a friend of Rihanna's, "and anyone who believes that is crazy!" Yet the craziness continued.

'Dem Haters' was a mirror for all of the strife Rihanna had been going through. She gave unsigned local Barbadian singer Dwane Husbands a featuring role on the song. An ex-janitor with a hidden passion for music whose singles had already been released on the island, he performed on the second verse. With this gesture, Rihanna wanted to prove she wasn't opposed to all Barbadians, just the ones that treated her unkindly and seemed to be against her.

Dwane's verse gave a warning not to let her enemies know how much she struggled. According to Rihanna, this was the story of her life. She hated to expose her weakness and vulnerability to others and kept it inside, not wanting to give people the satisfaction of knowing their slights bothered her.

She had kept the secret well. *Pop Matters* later enthused, "Yeah, it's a drag to have a hater in your circle, but you get the idea she's going to be OK. Rihanna just wanted to let you know, in case there was some hating going on in *your* camp. Now you'll know what to do with 'em." According to reviewers, then, she seemed untouchable – and that was just what she wanted. She had sung through her angst, but sealed her reputation as a tough girl at the same time.

The dark mood continued with 'Unfaithful', Rihanna's first big ballad. The concept for the song grew out of Rihanna's memories of her own infidelity as a 14-year-old in Barbados. "It wasn't a serious relationship, but I hid my infidelity for a long time," she admitted. "It got to the point where I knew he knew, so I had to tell him. I needed to get it out because I didn't want to be in the relationship anymore. I hated cheating, so it was a relief to admit it."

The song also seems to reference the film *Unfaithful*, starring Richard Gere, adding a darker, more dramatic edge to the story. The film told of a love triangle where a woman risks the solid, dependable relationship she has with her husband to embark on an exciting affair with a persuasive – but totally unsuitable – fling. Clandestine meetings and secretly snatched moments of passion follow, but things come to a head when her husband learns of her betrayal. Furious, he confronts her lover and, caught up in their heated exchange, he kills him.

In Rihanna's version, the macabre concept remained, but the roles were switched: not just another fickle teenage girl caught between the affections of two lovers, Rihanna wanted to cast herself in the role of the killer. "I'm referred to as [the] murderer in that song," she told MTV. "I'm taking this guy's life by hurting him, cheating on him. He knows and it makes him feel so bad. It's killing him to know that another guy is making me happy." She added, "I love that song, because we always put it out there than guys cheat and finally, someone put it in perspective. Girls cheat too."

Stargate were on board again for the track – but should Rihanna have been dubious? The Swedish duo had written for her before, but would a team responsible for the pre-teen bubblegum pop of 'S-Club Party' by S-Club 7 be the right choice for such dark subject matters? They had just propelled old-school crooner Lionel Richie back into the public eye with 'I Call It Love', his first R&B hit in 10 years' and were at the top of their game – but was it the game Rihanna wanted to play?

They were working on an album that she hoped would be tougher and representative of growing up as a girl whose life experiences had given her a harder edge. After all, Rihanna's childhood had never been about children's birthday parties or dreaming of a white wedding with the childhood sweetheart she would devote herself to for life. Her world was one of hard partying, domestic violence and crack cocaine addiction. Could Stargate measure up to what she had in mind? And if they didn't, was there anything she could do about it?

Once again, however, Stargate wouldn't disappoint her. Dramatic piano notes increased the tension in the atmosphere as she sang about her murderous betrayal – one that would leave her loved one's world crashing down.

There was another special guest in the studio for the track too – Ne-Yo. At the time, he had just broken onto the scene. Although he'd been writing and singing since the mid-1990s, it wasn't until he co-wrote a track called 'Let Me Love You' for another singer, Mario, that he became a name in the music industry. The song had been number one on the US *Billboard* charts for nine weeks at the beginning of 2005.

Rihanna heard his efforts and was instantly impressed. "I was like, 'Who the hell wrote this song?'" she recalled to MTV. "And everyone was like 'Ne-Yo, Ne-Yo, this kid Ne-Yo.' And one day, I was working in the studio on 'If It's Loving That You Want' and Ne-Yo stopped by. So we finally got to meet and he's like, 'Yeah, we've got to do something,' but we never got round to it on the first album. So for the second album, I was like, 'You know what? I have to work with that guy Ne-Yo.'"

Her persistence paid off and their collaboration on 'Unfaithful' would create a track she would later describe as one of her favourites on the album. She added, "He's one of the sweetest, sweetest people I've ever met, ever worked with."

With both Ne-Yo and Stargate on board, Rihanna was feeling confident about the album's success. She felt the same about 'We Ride', a heartbreak anthem that was also co-produced by Stargate. "'We Ride' is about this guy... promising all these things and then it turns out that he broke all of his promises, which is sad – but it's summer and I don't care," she explained to MTV. "If you want to do that, and be ugly and unfaithful, then I can just do my thing, chill with my girls and have fun." She added, "That's what summers are all about... every summer you remember a certain relationship and there's always a song to connect to that. So, 'We Ride' is just one of those songs."

Everyone from Justin Timberlake to Lady Gaga has written about summer love – Rihanna's version was just a little more twisted. Regrets, broken promises and bitterness – as well as moments of weakness longing for her lover to return – are all overcome by the prospect of a girly day out in the summer sun.

Due to Rihanna's jet-setting schedule, the album was recorded all over the world, including LA, New York and Barbados – but the most special recording destination for her was the location where 'Break It Off' was penned. She got together with Sean Paul, who had also appeared on Beyoncé's 'Baby Boy', for a dancehall collaboration in his native Jamaica. The song, which featured a lustful dialogue between two lovers hoping to hook up, was inspired in part by reggae legend Bob Marley.

"I have so much respect and love for Sean Paul," Rihanna told *Pop Matters* of her recording experience. "He took me to visit the Bob Marley museum before going into the studio, which was an amazing experience. When we finally got to the studio, I felt as though Marley's spirit was in the room with us." Indeed, the late singer's resting place was just a matter of miles away in the nearby village of Nine Mile.

Elsewhere on the album, the mood swiftly changes from the light-hearted lust of 'Break It Off' to full-blown obsession in songs such as 'Selfish Girl', where thoughts of her lover consume Rihanna night and day.

'Crazy Thing Called Love' follows a similar theme, echoing Beyoncé's 'Crazy In Love' or 'Dangerously In Love'. Just like Beyoncé, Rihanna is horrified to wake up one day and discover that she wants her man so much, she has lost both her sanity and her pride. Although Rihanna was not credited as a co-writer, the lyrics were personalised for her, featuring a dialogue between her and one of her best friends in real life, Leandra Griffith. J-Status also made an appearance to spice up the song.

Meanwhile, love doesn't get much more dangerous than on 'Final Goodbye', a modern-day Romeo and Juliet love story featuring a girl who would both live and die for her man – and prepares to breathe her last breath by his side.

Other love stories include 'PS I'm Still Not Over You', expressing regret at the loss of a perfect love, and 'A Million Miles Away', the tale of a dead relationship which has finally lost its spark, leaving only fake sentiment behind. Arguably, though, the most powerful song of the album is 'A Girl Like Me', which aimed to show off Rihanna's versatility. Not only had she mastered rock, reggae, dancehall and pop, but she had also recorded a smooth soul number that wouldn't have sounded out of place on a Craig David album. It captures the 'Can you handle all I have to give?' vibe of Destiny's Child's 'Bootylicious' – had its background been switched for a moody love song – while the hook echoes Craig David's 'Fill Me In'. Dreamy Spanish-sounding guitars complete the picture.

Here, Rihanna feels like a square peg in a round hole and is searching for a man who can take on and appreciate all that is different about her – all the things that separate her from the rest. It was a theme for the entire CD. "It's called *A Girl Like Me* because it's a very personal album," she told *Artist Direct*. "It's my baby. It's all about what it's like to be a girl like me, speaking of personal experiences as well as things that girls like me have gone through… there's some party lyrics. There's some relationship topics. There are some topics about keeping haters out of your circle. We go everywhere. Everything about me."

But the personal touch didn't extend to creative control in the studio. A bashful Rihanna had been holding back, preferring to let others make key decisions. When asked how much control she was given in song decisions and in recording, she told *MP3*, "As much as I want really. But I don't like to be too much in control and too dominant. I like to hear other people, get other people's opinions, because I respect other people's opinions, especially in the creative world. I get advice from producers."

Unfortunately, this confession gave ammunition to those who believed she was a puppet, under the control of executives in the showbiz world. If the website had been trying to trick her into admitting she was manufactured, she had fallen right into the trap. One anonymous critic claimed, "In one interview, Rihanna was asked which songs on the CD she thinks represent her as a person the best. She actually had to look out the track list before she could answer!"

However, putting her trust in the record company's judgement hadn't burned her badly so far. She had hated 'Pon De Replay' to begin with, but once she had got past her reservations and recorded it, the track had gone on to become a platinum-selling single. Perhaps Rihanna was still

Before the good girl went bad: Rihanna keeps it feminine with long hair and a flowery blouse as she poses in her hometown of St Michael, Barbados, to celebrate the April 22, 2006 release of second album *A Girl Like Me*. SCOTT GRIES/GETTY IMAGES

Rihanna gets her career off to a star-studded start at a Jay-Z hosted event at the Teen People Listening Lounge on July 24, 2005 in West Hollywood, California. KEVIN WINTER/GETTY IMAGES

Flying the flag for Barbados: Rihanna and her mentor Jay-Z strike a pose together at the 2005 Mercedes Benz Polo Challenge in Bridgehampton, Long Island, where she hosts a match sponsored by her native Barbados. JOHN ROCA/NY DAILY NEWS ARCHIVE VIA GETTY IMAGES

Rihanna experiments with style, showing off her Abercrombie & Fitch designer jeans paired with an Indian style jewelled hoodie, in Cologne in 2005 ROB VERHORST/REDFERNS

A thrilled Rihanna celebrates her platinum status success, with over a million albums sold, on the NBC *Today* show in New York on July 21, 2006 EVAN AGOSTINI/GETTY IMAGES

Family Girl: Rihanna shows her maternal side with her baby brother at New York's People Music Lounge on August 14, 2007. JOHNNY NUNEZ/WIREIMAGE

Feud forgotten: Rihanna reunites with her former drug addict father in time to celebrate her album launch for *A Girl Like Me* at the Hilton Hotel, Barbados. DAVID CRICHLOW/REX FEATURES

A picture of innocence: Rihanna clutches a beach-ball and leans in for an early photo with fellow teen sensation Chris Brown. A few years later their picture perfect romance would dissolve into tragedy.

Rihanna poses with her MTV trophy at the Europe Music Awards in Denmark on November 2, 2006. At first sight a generic R&B diva, she dares to be different with a defiant flash of subversive black nail varnish

finding her own feet and, at the tender age of 18, wasn't yet ready to take control of her own destiny.

Instead, she threw herself into preparing for the album. At that stage, a series of lucrative sponsorship deals were arranged, which critics complained would "further erode" her identity. From now on, at a time when she was still discovering who she was, she would be touting Nike sportswear, JC Penney jeans and Nokia mobile phones – one of which appeared in the video for the album's lead single 'S.O.S'. Was Rihanna just a billboard on which to hang brand names – or an artist in her own right?

Three promotional videos were shot for 'S.O.S'. One was for the lingerie brand Agent Provocateur, and featured a hotel that transforms itself into a nightclub the moment Rihanna walks in. The second, for Nike, appealed to viewers' competitive instincts by depicting a dance competition in a gym. An interactive work-out video with Rihanna's choreographer James King was downloadable, teaching how to recreate her dance moves. The video advertised a newly-launched range of dancewear for the company.

Finally, an official video was produced for the music stations, featuring Rihanna in a school locker room. Even that version proved to be full to the brim with advertising, showing Rihanna clutching a Nokia 3250 phone, which she uses to call for help when her love-struck emotions get the better of her, and listening to an MP3 of Soft Cell's original track 'Tainted Love'.

All three videos had one thing in common – although Rihanna was singing about a love interest who drove her crazy, outwardly she was an image of polished perfection. Tweaked by a team of on-set make-up artists and stylists, she was anything but out of control. What was more, her single got off to a flying start after its release on March 7, 2006, providing Rihanna with her first ever stateside number one. It also hit the top spot in Australia and the second spot in both the UK and Germany. Overall, it went on to sell more than four million copies worldwide.

But the biggest test was yet to come. Rihanna had thrown herself into preparations for the album, including interviews, promo tours, rehearsals, vocal training, intensive choreography sessions, workouts and, of course, her dreaded school-work assignments. The day of reckoning came in April, when *A Girl Like Me* finally hit the shops. She needn't have been worried, though. Its first-week sales doubled that of *Music Of The Sun* with 115,000 copies sold. It reached number one in Canada and number five in the UK.

However, her upgrade really came into focus on September 8, when she performed at Fashion Rocks, a high-octane, style-packed event that kicks off New York's Fall Fashion Week each year. Although Beyoncé, Christina Aguilera and The Scissor Sisters all made an appearance, Rihanna's fans contested that she stole the show with her duet with Elton John, covering his classic song 'The Bitch Is Back'. The same week, her new fashion education gave her a chance to outdo the unwaveringly glamorous Beyoncé when the two were photographed together at the latter's birthday party.

At that time, Beyoncé was still the hottest R&B artist around – and was winning the awards to prove it – but Rihanna was quickly gaining ground. At the previous month's Video Music Awards on August 31, she had earned two nominations in both the Best New Artist and Viewer's Choice categories.

Plus, although she had been beaten to the top spot on both occasions, she had celebrated the mentions with a brand new tattoo. In fact, her obsession with body art was her favourite way to unwind. "When I am in New York, after all the photo shoots and performances, when I should be resting, sometimes I get dressed and go to the tattoo parlours in SoHo and hang out," she confessed. "I am so intrigued by tattoos. It's an entire culture and I study it."

To celebrate the nominations, she and her best friend, Melissa Forde, whom she had had jetted in from Barbados, had descended on the city to get matching friendship symbols inked behind their right ears. "We had to do something crazy," Rihanna explained.

Meanwhile, the style lessons might have been too much too soon when, at the event itself, Rihanna slipped on her precariously high heels and went flying. Six-inch heels were a whole new world for a former tomboy not used to wearing anything higher than flats in public.

However, the next day it was business as usual, with Rihanna posing in a long, pastel pink dress for acclaimed photographer David LaChapelle. A team of make-up artists plumped up her pout with a selection of no fewer than 38 cosmetics brushes, and Rihanna entertained herself by giving Kanye West a back massage – these days it was all in a day's work.

While she was living it up on the road, 'Unfaithful', which had been officially released on July 17, was climbing the charts fast. It peaked at number six in the States and number two in the UK, losing only to Shakira and Wyclef Jean's Latin-themed number 'Hips Don't Lie'. The song went on to sell over 4.5 million copies.

Hot on its heels was the anthemic 'We Ride', released on August 21. It was more light-hearted than its predecessor, coupling the fickle and flighty aspects of teenage relationships instead of the more intense ones. Agonising over whether there was still a chance for her and the lover who fell out of her favour, Rihanna soon cheers up when her friends suggest a day out in the sunshine, after which all is forgotten.

The video, shot in the Florida Keys, followed the same plot. Unusually for a girl who had prided herself on having "three girl friends and about three million guy friends", she claimed the theme of the video was a quick recovery from her heartbreak: "It's OK, because I've got my girls with me." The video portrayed a summer-fun vibe but, according to Rihanna, the reality was very different. "I'm dancing, like technical dance, which was a challenge," she told MTV. "It usually takes years to learn, but we got it done in a few days."

The reward for her hard work was seeing two of her singles near the top of the charts at the same time. 'We Ride' failed to reach the heights of 'Unfaithful' but it too was a success.

Meanwhile, Rihanna's fans in the US were getting to see another side of her talents at home on TV. All of the drama of the past few years in the public eye had left Rihanna well prepared for a sideline in acting, and she had first appeared in an episode of the TV series *All My Children*, sliding down a red carpet and performing her own songs in a fictional nightclub. Although her performance wasn't too far removed from real life by that time, it whetted her appetite for acting, particularly in the movies. She was desperate for a challenge and longed to work with people like Jessica Alba, but she recognised that she had to start small and debuted, again as herself, in the straight-to-DVD movie *Bring It On: All Or Nothing.*

The cheerleading drama, featuring Beyoncé's sister Solange Knowles, is a riches-to-rags tale centring around a wealthy, pretty and popular cheer captain called Britney who, as far as teenage girls' worlds go, appears to have it all. Then her father is made redundant, forcing the family to move to a seedier part of town. She reluctantly joins a rival cheerleading team at her new school and the two opposing teams then go head to head for a chance to appear in Rihanna's music video. While Britney's well-to-do ex-classmates sneer at her performance, branding it 'ghetto', it is the one that wins Rihanna's approval and it is her team that are chosen to appear in the new version of 'Pon De Replay', created specifically for the film. Solange and her classmates dance in the background as Rihanna sings out the chorus.

"I never really had to act," she chuckled to *Interview* magazine later. "I was just basically being myself. This is the first time I've had a [film] role, I actually had to do something that I had to get prepared for. I didn't know if I was going to like or hate it or love it. But I actually enjoy it." However, she was adamant that the silver screen would not take over her career, adding, "I'll never shut off from music and just do film. I love music too much."

She proved the point when she returned to the studio yet again to record a new single, 'Roll It', with J-Status and old friend Shontelle, the song's co-writer. The tune had originally started life in Barbados and was released by a local singer, Alison Hinds. The original lyrics had talked of religion, self-respect and feminist empowerment, boasting down-to-earth values such as getting a degree, nurturing children and keeping a God-fearing lifestyle. When it was adapted for J-Status however, it offered sizzling sex appeal and was transformed into a full-blown musical threesome.

Where the original talks of belief in God, the J-Status version has writhing and hip-shaking to calypso – as mentioned earlier, a genre strictly forbidden by the church. While Alison preaches against abusing your body, J-Status and Rihanna promote sexual freedom.

Another song with mixed messages was 'Winning Women', a joint effort between Rihanna and Pussycat Doll Nicole Scherzinger, created to promote the new Secret deodorant. The song starts off as a feminist anthem, talking of emotional strength, financial independence and trading on the stock exchange. However, by the end, the lyrics assert that all a girl needs is the simple life and the love of a good man. Perhaps the aim was to appeal to both the kept woman and the independent woman at the same time.

Soon after, Rihanna teamed up with The Pussycat Dolls again, supporting them on their UK tour. The shows, which would culminate at London's Wembley Arena, pitted Rihanna's most recent single, 'We Ride', against the Dolls' latest effort, 'I Don't Need A Man', and was aimed at diversifying her audience.

Rihanna also supported her mentor Jay-Z for three dates in South Africa and briefly joined his headlining Roc Tha Block tour that year, appearing as support across North America for acts such as The Black Eyed Peas. It might have seemed as though Rihanna was always the bridesmaid and never the bride with all of these support slots, most of which saw her perform for a meagre 30 minutes per night. However, it was earning her valuable exposure – a tactic that would pay off when it came to that year's most prestigious award ceremonies. Thus far, Rihanna had struggled to gain success in her own right or to be seen as more than just the manufactured creation of a man who many felt wanted to mould her into a baby Beyoncé. Yet the days of being in Beyoncé's shadow might have been over.

At the MTV Europe Music Awards in Copenhagen, held on November 2, 2006, Rihanna wowed *The Mirror*, who reported, "Move over, Beyoncé, hot young babe Rihanna is now the new voice and body of R&B... before scooping the award for best R&B act, the 18-year-old braved the icy temperatures on the red carpet... giving a heartstoppingly sexy performance of 'S.O.S.'."

It was a similar story on November 15, when she jetted to London for the World Music Awards. The ceremony would prove to be very special because, although no-one knew it at the time, it would be Michael Jackson's last live performance. Fellow R&B artist Chris

Brown performed a cover of 'Thriller' in his honour. Rihanna was due to take to the stage directly after Michael gave his acceptance speech for the coveted Diamond Award – a tall order for any artist to follow due to Jackson's legendary status – but she still received rave reviews from *The Mirror*, who insisted "Sorry, Beyoncé, but Rihanna was the real star."

Rihanna finally beat Beyoncé to an award when she won Female Artist of the Year at the American *Billboard* Awards on December 5 in Las Vegas. Beyoncé, who had also been nominated for the category, was left to trail behind as one of the runners up. "I can't feel my legs!" Rihanna gasped. "This is phenomenal." Her surprise was understandable. In just over a year, she had managed to surpass a woman who had been on the music scene for more than a decade. Was she a credible threat to her rival's throne already?

To her fans, one thing that set her apart from Beyoncé, six years her senior, was her insatiable youth, her ability to relate to the teen market and provide a voice that expressed what they felt, and her crystal-clear memories of the topsy-turvy heart-in-a-blender style emotions of young love affairs. As yet, she was less pristine and polished than Beyoncé – raw, but also a little more accessible.

She had barely had time to recover from the elation of her victory before 'Break It Off', her duet with Sean Paul, hit the airwaves. It was released on December 14 as a digital download without so much as a music video to accompany it; but in spite of its modest promotion, it peaked at number nine on the US singles chart.

Challenging the critics who claimed her success was down to the long list of high-profile names she shared her album with, it now looked as though Rihanna was about to outshine her more established singing partner. According to *Pop Matters*, "When Paul works his magic, he threatens to steal all the shine, but Rihanna's hook is so infectious that hers is the voice you ultimately remember."

On New Year's Eve 2007, the pair performed it live together. The show coincided with a turning point for Rihanna. Now that she had the success she had strived for, she wanted to ride the waves on her own terms. Her thoughts were no longer consumed with getting a song in the charts alone, but on the message she would give when she got there.

On 'A Girl Like Me', she had wanted someone who could let her be herself, but increasingly, she felt her efforts to do that had been knocked back by those anxious to control her sound, image and lyrics. As the 16-year-old desperate for a record deal, whom Evan Rogers had described as "painfully shy", she hadn't questioned her managers' decisions. Now, however, it was time to start living out her own lyrics. It was time for a good girl to go bad.

Chapter 4

Dancing in the Rain

"I hold this bitch responsible for the wettest summer ever in the UK! This summer has been so fucking ridiculous – torrential rain, people drowned, the whole lot – and this bitch has been at number one in our pop charts for *nine weeks*!" raged one internet forum member. "I think it's a rain dance and she wants it to rain – that's why she's always singing about umbrellas!"

Rihanna might have been warming to the bad girl role, but was she really responsible for thunderstorms, severe weather warnings and flash floods? According to an indignant nation, the answer was yes. It had all begun at the end of 2006, long before Rihanna's rain dances hit the public eye. She had been about to start recording sessions for her new album. But, fed up with conforming to the look of a sweet, innocent teenager, she informed anyone who would listen that she needed a change. Album number three would feature a girl with a completely different lifestyle.

Yet Rihanna's management were gobsmacked when they learnt that her main inspiration came from Amy Winehouse. It didn't bode well. At the time, Amy was already more likely to be found face down in a pool of vomit than in a recording studio. Had Rihanna's team spent months fine-tuning her image for maximum glamour only for her to turn into a woman who regularly topped the worst-dressed lists of the world's tabloids?

Amy might have been rock'n'roll, but her excesses weren't exactly music to the ears of industry bosses. To them, there was a fine line between publicity-touting debauchery and downright self-destruction – and many would argue that Amy crossed it. What was more, she was more famous for not changing her clothes for five days in a row than for any burgeoning sense of style.

When she did remember to get dressed, she made sure she was as scantily clad as possible – some branded her look 'trashy'. What could it be about her that had Rihanna so enthused – just when her label thought they'd nailed her trademark image?

It certainly wasn't drug shopping lists that appealed to her. After witnessing her father's meltdown, she had promised she'd never do a hard drug as long as she lived. Moreover, it wasn't blackened fingernails or unkempt beehives that Rihanna – previously one of R&B's slickest stars – had in mind either. It was the freedom to be who she was – and in Rihanna's world, that liberty was sorely lacking.

"I love Amy," Rihanna told *Monsters and Critics*. "She's so real. She's like, 'This is who I am – whatever.'" She was impressed by her refusal to paint a picture of polished perfection for the benefit of the cameras and her disdain for consulting those in authority before she did something. Sure, she had bleached her hair an acidic shade of peroxide blonde, which the tabloids described as "hideous" – but she hadn't needed to ask anyone's permission to go left-field. Her success hadn't been built up from toeing the line.

To Rihanna, Amy wasn't fake or false and she wasn't looking for approval. She expected followers to like her look and behaviour, or lump it. If her audience criticised her, she was prone to simply calling them "monkey cunts". While Rihanna wasn't about to go that far, she knew she needed a change.

Rihanna was growing concerned that her look was no different and no more edgy than any of the other girls that were flooding the pop industry. Christina Milian, Mariah Carey, Ciara and Beyoncé – all mixed-race women that you'd find in the R&B section of your local HMV – seemed to her to be conforming to the same style.

They all had long hair that they had experimented with by dyeing it blonde. To her, long bleached-blonde hair, an innocent smile and a look that was the epitome of pretty wouldn't distinguish her from any other female in the game – and what's more, she didn't want to play that part. It just wasn't her.

Rihanna not only felt that the generic pop star look was "boring", but that women of colour like herself were betraying their roots by turning to Western ideals of beauty to ensure they remained in the public eye. She didn't believe that their look matched who they were or what they felt inside.

In a moment of rebellion, Rihanna decided her own long locks had to go. During a day off in Paris, she sneaked into the nearest hair salon and had her hair chopped into a short, sleek bob. She was over the moon with the result – but not for long. "The minute I got back, someone in authority was like, 'Yeah, your hair looks good,'" she told *The Observer*. "But somebody else went, 'You need to put your hair back in – soon.'"

The disapproval stopped a confused Rihanna in her tracks. "It just crushed me. When you're growing up, 17, 18, that's when you're really trying to figure out who you are and at that point, I just wanted to try something outside of the box," she continued. "But as soon as you come out of your shell, like, 'This is who I am,' they just shove you back in with, 'No, because this is what we want the box to look like.' You just feel like a tool after a while."

Silently accepting it at first, Rihanna eventually began to ask questions. "I was like, 'What do you mean, I can't cut my hair? It has to be long and blonde, like every other female singer in the game?' No, I'm not doing that."

It was the beginning of a battle of wills between Rihanna and her label. "I felt like the whole world had long, curly, flowing blonde hair," she lamented to *The Guardian*. "[But] they made me put my long hair back in [as extensions]."

She also rejected the carefully controlled rules that applied to her make-up. "There were a lot of restraints on what I could do," she groaned to *Glamour*. "I couldn't wear certain colours of lipstick, like bright pink, dark pink or red – my lips had to be natural." She recalled that, while making her first album, she had been so grateful for the opportunity of fame that she hadn't even questioned her manufactured role. By the time she had started recording the second, she had grown out of the girl-next-door demeanour and had finally figured out who she wanted to be. Yet even then, according to a frustrated Rihanna, "I still wasn't allowed to do it."

"In the beginning it was almost like I was just going along with a script that was written for me and I didn't feel like an artist – I felt like a tool," she told *The Observer*. "I just felt like, 'Hey, here I am, this money-making vehicle for this big record label and I'm not even having fun, I'm not enjoying it, because I'm not able to be who I am... Then, finally, I said, 'You know what? If I want to do this, I'm going to do it my way!'"

Rihanna cut her hair, dyed it jet black, and threw her extensions away for good. She hadn't consulted her management, feeling they wouldn't understand or, even worse, might try to stop her.

"I basically took the attitude of the bad girl and I got really rebellious and just did everything the way I wanted to do it," she told *Entertainment Weekly*. "I didn't want to listen to anybody. I didn't consult with anybody. I just want to have a little more fun and be a little more experimental with my image... I just reinvented myself."

Now that the world's newspapers were following her, being like everyone else wasn't enough. She couldn't stand the thought of having a look that was clichéd – she had tried that as a child. "She had these really long dreads that people would compliment her on," a friend says of Rihanna's youth. "And even though it's true that she did [wear] a lot of sports clothes, it was always in a feminine way. I remember seeing a lot of pastel colours. I think she was under a lot of peer pressure, because there were so many feminine girls at the school and she wanted to fit in. But it's obvious now that wasn't her at all."

Perhaps her style evolution was natural, especially as – like most teenagers – she despised being told what to do. She later told *Entertainment Weekly*, "I was being forced into a particular innocent image and I just had to break away from that. I think every teenager just has a point in their lives when they just get rebellious. They go into their own world, they shut everybody's opinion out and they don't care. That's when they stick to what they want and that's what I'm doing now."

She was about to show the world the rebel side of her – the one her grandmother had warned everyone about. Her ruthless style-overhaul extended to her music as well – she rejected her trademark reggae crossover sound. With her island rhythms, she had found a winning formula that had brought her money, fame and success; but if she wanted to be herself, that would have to go as well. There was not a trace of reggae, soca or dancehall on her third album. "[To my label], it had to be safe, and in order for it to be safe, it had to have been done before, which made no sense to me," she complained to *The Observer*.

She didn't want to be marketed as having purely a Caribbean sound, but she didn't want to become a replica of a British or American girl group either. What she had in mind, somewhere between the two, might not have been conventional for the industry, but with her two years of success, Rihanna felt she had paid her dues and was entitled to experiment.

According to ex-Combermere pupil Paul Browne, not only was it just a personal choice, but it also made sound financial sense. "Am I disappointed that she turned away from reggae? In a word, no," he told the author. "I think if Rihanna had stayed with her original sound, she would have ended up in obscurity like many international artists. The big challenge is always to make it in America – and white America at that."

Fortunately, Rihanna had the support of two very important mentors for her new sound. Jay-Z had just finished promoting his own album, *Kingdom Come*, and was now taking a break from his own career to focus fully on promoting the talent he had signed from behind the scenes. He had the time to indulge Rihanna, allowing her to explore new facets of herself under his wing. "It's a fortunate position for all of us," he told MTV. "[My protégés] benefit from my years of experience in the music business, and I benefit from their fresh, new energy and their talent. It's a two-way street."

Video director Chris Applebaum also approved, feeling Rihanna's sound couldn't be categorised. "She's unclassifiable," he said. "You can't say she's strictly R&B or pop. She's more of an impresario."

Another of Jay-Z's artists, Ne-Yo, gave Rihanna her first-ever voice lessons. "He is such a genius," she enthused to MTV. "I've never had vocal training, so when I'm in the studio, he'll tell me how to breathe and stuff. And I'm like, 'What?' Like, he'll call out these big fancy words – 'OK, I want you to do staccato.' And I'm like, 'OK, I don't know what that is!'"

After her technical training, she teamed up with Ne-Yo again, when he co-wrote and dueted with her on 'Hate That I Love You'. Another Stargate production, the song is a big ballad similar to their previous effort, 'Unfaithful'. However, Rihanna's stamp is on the song as, once again, it is about twisted rather than conventional love.

The bubblegum sound and softly spoken words might tug at the heart-strings, but it's no ordinary love song – underneath it all is the love-hate message encapsulated in the song's title. The couple are frustrated by their fluctuating relationship in which, no matter what the other does, all is forgiven with a glimpse of an irresistible smile. When Rihanna first heard it, she was blown away by the psychological aspects of the song – if a little confused.

"I read through the lyrics and I was like, 'What are you thinking? What's going through your head?'" Rihanna recalled to MTV. "I just have to stop sometimes and be like, 'Ne-Yo, OK, tell me why you wrote this song.' Because I don't understand how he comes up with certain concepts and he just blows me away sometimes. He's just insane." She added, "When it starts off, you think it's a sexy song but you have to listen to the lyrics. It's a really deep song."

The same could be said of another song with an ambiguous meaning that Ne-Yo co-wrote for her, 'Question Existing'. Beginning with a graphic description of a girl undressing, at first it sounds like the cheeky masturbation anthem 'Oops (Oh My)' by Tweet, or the mild titillation of a phone-sex advert, but – despite its misleading start – it quickly reveals a deeper side. Rihanna, using her real name, Robyn, confides in her diary about the perils of fame, the superficial relationships and the media intrusion that follows. According to Rihanna, being surrounded by *faux* friends in the spotlight could be very lonely – her biggest challenge being to separate those attracted to her fame and those who want to be her friend for who she really is.

One studio employee told the author, "That trickery was deliberate, to add an edge to the song. It starts off very cute and sexy, but you're drawn into this murky world of fame instead. Listening to it lyrically, it's like thinking you're having consensual sex with a woman, only to find she's actually a trafficked prostitute and very unhappy. All is not what it seems in the world of fame."

He added, "I think it's a metaphor for what it's like going into fame in the first place. You think it'll all be roses, with people adoring you wherever you go, and then off come the rose-tinted glasses and the sinister side comes out, which is just a world of insults and put-downs. Not being able to go out for a meal without the paparazzi following behind you, and every mistake you make being in public. It's not that easy.

"She might be doing a job that seems just a bit of fun, but underneath this stage image is a real person who has real feelings too, and, just like everyone else, she can get hurt. I have dated famous women because of this industry and, let me tell you, the supposed glamour of this job offers no immunity. It's a harsh world out there, maybe even especially if you're famous. There's so much more expected of you."

Yet the pressure on Rihanna was reduced by the stable of top producers working for her. Ne-Yo in particular, she said, knew "exactly how to put into words how I feel." But she was equally pleased with a trio of songs produced by Timbaland – 'Sell Me Candy', 'Lemme Get That' and 'Rehab' – and with the fact that the first two had a more exotic sound than the rest of the album, bringing in Caribbean and Indian influences to the mix.

'Sell Me Candy' starts off as a casual summer fling – fleetingly addictive but nothing serious – in the thematic style of Lady Gaga's 'Boys Boys Boys'. The lyrics talk of candy melting in her hands, sparking an innuendo-fest that would later inspire Katy Perry in 'California Girls', where she talks of women so hot they'll melt an admirer's 'popsicle'. However, things soon spiral so much out of control for Rihanna that she no longer wants to buy into a fantasy of a rock'n'roll summer romance, but merely wants love and to live for each other – a sentiment delivered in a silky and sensual Bollywood style. Timbaland had been experimenting with Indian themes on his own album, *Shock Value*, and 'Sell Me Candy' became a natural extension of that.

If Rihanna was sweet like candy then she transformed into a hardened pro just in time for 'Lemme Get That', a rhythmic chant with a distinctly African sound. As materialistic as Beyoncé's 'Upgrade You' and as audacious as Katy Perry's 'If You Can Afford Me', it shows Rihanna on a mission for her and her boyfriend to become the king and queen of the music scene – with a long string of assets to prove it. The song is a shameless and defiant ode to greed and purchase fever, name-checking Gucci and Mercedes Benz in the process. Her boyfriend might have sex on his mind, but Rihanna's is filled with very different thoughts, such as getting new furniture. It's a tale of manipulating her sex appeal to get what she wants. The theme was new territory to the more moralistic Rihanna, who confessed, "It's so not me, but it's kind of me going into a character and playing a character."

And while the good girl had definitely gone bad, underneath the risqué new image was a hint of traditional Caribbean values – ones that told her that prostituting herself for designer handbags and top-of-the-range yachts might be taking things a little too far. She told *The Observer*, "I think the American way is a fantasy. People live with air in their head, really. Their priorities in life are fancy cars and bling. In Barbados, it's all about having fun, definitely, but also about having good grades."

Rihanna felt she had scored the best grades she could get when she managed to organise a recording slot with Justin Timberlake. She claimed to have felt "very blessed, definitely favoured by God" when the two got together with Timbaland for the song 'Rehab'.

She had been fitting in recording sessions with Timbaland's busy touring schedule, which saw him take to the stage with Justin every night. After one show in Chicago, Justin was jamming in the studio, trying to style a new beat – but Rihanna had made such an impression on him that, by the time he returned to New York, he told her he wanted the song to be hers. Timbaland, who knew instantly he wanted to call the song 'Rehab', collaborated to create the beat. "Then Justin came in and he just put his thing on," Rihanna told *Entertainment Weekly*. "He wrote the song in his head. He didn't write anything on paper. He went into the booth and sang it and I was very impressed."

In the song, Rihanna plays the role of a distraught girl whose boyfriend gave her the strength to battle all of her addictions, replacing her bad habits with him. However, when she discovers that he was merely using her and the relationship cannot last, she ends up in rehab for a very different reason – to break her addiction to him.

"It's a metaphorical song," Rihanna explained to *Entertainment Weekly*. "'Rehab' really just means we have to get over the guy. So we talk about checking ourselves into rehab, meaning we have to get over him, and we compare the guy to a disease or an addiction. We're just saying, 'We don't want to smoke any cigarettes no more,' meaning we don't want to deal with this bullshit anymore."

Other than collaborations with top producers, Rihanna also had another ambition for the album – to make a foray into the world of rock. She had flirted with rock sounds on 'Kisses Don't Lie', and now she wanted to perform a much heavier number. That song was 'Shut Up And Drive'. Packed full of sexual innuendos, the throbbing, pulsating beats – aided by a sample of New Order's 'Blue Monday' – pushes forward images of a newly confident Rihanna. Now, she just needs someone who can take on the challenge of keeping up with her. *AllMusic* would later describe the song as a "sleek forthcoming proposition… as undeniable and rocking as the Sugababes' 2002 UK smash 'Freak Like Me'." Incidentally, the latter also borrowed vintage electronic sounds, sampling a Gary Numan song. However, the Sugababes' effort still retained a pop shine, while Rihanna hoped her track would have a harder edge.

'Push Up On Me' was another reflection of the new Rihanna, describing a hormone-driven fantasy about a man's sex appeal. He might be elusive and playing hard to get, but here Rihanna seems to court the challenge. She wants to conquer the unconquerable. The unusual choice of backdrop to this struggle is a sample of the 1983 Lionel Richie track, 'Running With The Night'.

The gentle side to Rihanna returns on 'Say It', where she urges a man to abandon his pride and not be afraid to be honest if it's commitment he wants from her. Talking of being able to find heaven if the two search together, it was the only track that Rihanna believed slightly suited the "cliché category".

But she was back to her newfound daredevil self with 'Breaking Dishes'. Whoever coined the phrase "revenge is a dish best served cold" certainly hadn't told Rihanna. When her boyfriend stays out late, she is burning up with rage, whether she is smashing plates or burning clothes. The most formidable fire of all, of course, is Rihanna's anger. To add a more sinister twist to the storyline, breaking glasses and plates was her way as a child of distracting her father from being physically violent in the home. Had she inherited his volatile temper?

If so, she was ready for the controversy. "[Being] a bad girl, it's all about the attitude that you take towards things – I'm not being careful, I'm just having fun," she told *Star Phoenix*. "I'm taking risks because bad girls take risks."

Meanwhile, she had done the broody ballads, the smooth R&B numbers and the classic Caribbean rhythms. Now she was ready for an up-tempo club anthem that would have everyone on the dancefloor. That track turned out to be 'Don't Stop The Music'.

Rihanna had initially been inspired by Brandy's album, *Afrodisiac*. To her, it was a CD full of floor-fillers, songs that were so infectiously catchy that she felt every one had the potential to be a single. "That album I listen to all day, all night," she enthused. "When I was in the studio, that was the album I listened to all the time and I really admired that every song was a great song and I was like, 'You know what? I have to make an album like this!'"

Her other inspiration was Michael Jackson, who she believed had never made a filler track in his entire career history. His stamp was added to the song when a sample of 'Wanna Be Startin' Somethin'' was woven in.

The final track was 'Good Girl Gone Bad', a cautionary tale to any man thinking of mistreating his woman. Tiring of finding women's phone numbers in his boyfriend's jacket pocket and waiting for him at home while he cruises the nightclubs, Rihanna's character leaves with his best friend as an act of revenge. No longer playing the housewife role, she's partying instead.

However, Rihanna was quick to point out that while she might have been bad, she wasn't debauched. "Bad is not sleazy," she corrected an interviewer on *Capital FM*. "Bad has its own term to every individual and in my case, it just means I've gotten a little rebellious on the album, broken out of my shell and I'm taking risks in a Michael Jackson 'Bad' kind of way."

The song represented liberation to her, having finally gained the courage to admit who she was – and she felt so strongly about the theme that it became the title of the CD. "We figured *Good Girl Gone Bad* was the perfect title because it showed people I'm my own person now, not doing what anyone wants me to do. I'm not the innocent Rihanna anymore. I'm taking a lot more chances," she told MTV. "I felt when I cut my hair, it shows people I'm not trying to be anyone else."

For someone who had been burdened with sponsorships and pre-rehearsed PR quotes, this was her way of breaking free. She had been the face of the Barbados Tourism Authority, starring in their TV adverts to tempt visitors – especially families – to the island for a holiday. That heaped enormous pressure on Rihanna to look like a poster girl for wholesome, family-friendly glamour – something that would appeal to holiday-makers with impressionable young children on board. Later that year, she would become an official ambassador for her country, with all the responsibility that it brought. She had also just landed a contract to be the new face of Covergirl in the USA, an ultra-feminine line of beauty products. Yet it seemed that Rihanna couldn't care less about the prospect of losing lucrative sponsorships if the cost was not being true to herself. In fact, she was ready to go to war to be herself.

That wasn't to say that she didn't enjoy her moments in the limelight with companies like Covergirl, though – it was the perfect contrast to her day job as the archetypal tough girl.

"It's a lot of fun being a Covergirl because I'm so against being too girly," she explained to *Concrete Loop*. "That keeps me in touch with my girly side because I like to be so hardcore sometimes and anti-innocent… Now [Covergirl] really keeps me in touch with my feminine side, I feel fun again, and it's fun playing around with the make-up."

Rihanna's identity as a tomboy with an occasional penchant for something more feminine was set, and her third album was almost ready. Yet, despite having secured almost a dozen credible pop tracks, Rihanna's team still felt that there was something missing – that one stand-out single that would make the CDs fly off the shelves. Their prayers were answered in the form of 'Umbrella'.

The track was borne out of a moment of boredom when producer Tricky Stewart had been playing with the free music-software program Garage Band, which was included on all Apple Mac computers. He started half-heartedly experimenting, until he came across a hi-hat sound that had co-producer Terius Nash jumping out of his seat. He immediately applied some chords to the sound and, within a matter of hours, they had what they thought was a potential chart-topper – all from a song that had started out as an accident. They then worked against the clock to sell it.

This was the song that Rihanna would later describe as "the highlight of my career" – but, originally destined for Britney Spears, it almost bypassed her altogether. Tricky Stewart had been desperate to give Britney a number one with the track, but, fortunately for Rihanna, Britney was going into career meltdown at the time and allegedly wasn't sober enough to listen to it, let alone record it. Tricky had worked with her on her previous album, *In The Zone*, and was keen to repeat his success with the next one, the perhaps appropriately named *Blackout*.

However, he was quickly pushed back by Britney's team, who claimed they already had several single-worthy tracks but were finding it difficult to get her inside the studio. As she was struggling to record the songs they already had, taking on more was out of the question. "Her current state was a little bizarre," Tricky recalled to MTV of the setback. "It wasn't meant to be."

Disappointed, he and Terius immediately wracked their brains to find another suitable artist to send it to. The weekend of the 2007 Grammy Awards was upon them and Mary J. Blige was the standout artist, nominated for eight gongs. They sent it to her and, as an afterthought, mailed a copy to Rihanna. She would not be nominated for any categories at that year's Grammys and was merely co-hosting the ceremony.

Although Mary stopped short of delivering an all-out rejection, she was busy with her pre-Grammy commitments and wasn't available to give the track her seal of approval. Rihanna's team was interested, but Tricky and Terius were more inclined to sign it over to the bigger star, the one with a string of award nominations to her name. However much Rihanna might have fallen in love with the song, she had some serious competition on her hands.

"At the time, if you heard Mary's name and you heard Rihanna's name, you'd want to hold out," Tricky admitted to MTV. "Mary's coming off *Be Without You*, she's nominated for all these Grammys, the whole thing. So the plan with us, really, was to hold the record to get a response from Mary."

Rihanna knew what she was up against, telling *The Daily Telegraph*, "Any songwriter would die for her to sing one of their songs, so I just prayed that we got it. It was perfect for me – it had a West Indian groove." What was more, the sound was growing on her fast. "When the demo first started playing, I was like, 'This is interesting, this is weird...' But the song kept getting better. I listened to it over and over. I said, 'I need this record. I need to record it tomorrow.'"

It had developed from an innocent professional interest to a full-blown obsession – and Tricky was thrown into what he would describe as "the bidding war of our lives".

However, the most enthusiastic campaigner was Rihanna herself. No longer hiding behind her more experienced management, she hunted Terius Nash down herself at the Grammys, and told him she meant business. She wanted that song and she wasn't taking no for an answer.

"No-one wants to be teased," she huffed to *The Guardian*. "How can you bring a record to me when you took it to a million people at the same time? I thought Mary J. Blige was going to get it for sure. But at the back of my mind, I was thinking, 'No, wait, I'm never giving this up.' I went up to the guy at the Grammys and I was like "Umbrella' is mine' and he just kind of giggled. And I really held his face, like, 'No, you're not hearing me, 'Umbrella' is *my* record!'"

The pair still hadn't heard back from Mary – and playing it to artists such as Taio Cruz and Akon had proved fruitless too. Their options were decreasing by the minute, while Rihanna's team seemed to have started a campaign of mild harassment against them.

"By the time L.A. Reid and his team get done beating us up, we just couldn't say 'No,'" Tricky chuckled to MTV. "They're calling every 20 minutes for the entire Grammy weekend. Every time we see him, everywhere we see him, they were just applying all kinds of pressure."

Tricky was still unconvinced that Rihanna was the right woman for the song, but her team weren't exactly playing hard to get and, finally, he reluctantly decided to sign the song over to her. Within two days of writing it, he was in a recording studio in LA watching her put her own stamp on the track.

As soon as he heard her version of the 'ella' refrain in the chorus, there were dollar signs in his eyes. "When she recorded the 'ellas', you knew it was about to be the jump-off," he recalled, "and your life was about to change if you had anything to do with that record."

Mary J. Blige was no longer one of those people. When she finally had a chance to properly hear the song, she was just as keen – but it was too late. "They did the song for me," Mary told MTV. "It was during the Grammy time and I was really, really busy and I heard it and I was like, 'Oh my goodness, that's a smash! I love this song!' And it was like, 'It's yours.' So, in the midst of it being mine, they were probably telling Rihanna that it was hers." To dampen down the rumours of bad feeling, she added, "She's such a beautiful lady and I love her to death. I was so glad that she caught it."

There was even more good news in store for Rihanna, who felt like the cat that got the cream. Unbeknown to her, Jay-Z had been recording his own vocal to incorporate into her song. "They just said, 'We have a surprise for you,'" Rihanna recalled to MTV. "I couldn't imagine it would be Jay-Z getting in on the song. They played it for me and I had goosebumps everywhere. I still can't believe that… it takes everything to another level for me in my career as far as experience goes."

Rihanna might have been surprised, but that was nothing compared to Tricky's reaction when Jay-Z unexpectedly changed the lyrics on his verse just before the official recordings began. He was gobsmacked. "There was another version before that one that he did and the first one was perfect," Tricky told MTV. "Right before they were about to press it up, he went and changed his verse – and nobody even knew… At the time when he did it, I didn't really understand it. But now, when I go back once in a while and listen to the old rap, what we wrote about makes so much better sense [with the new rap] and, from a songwriter's standpoint, he just really made it more about the song, with the metaphors about umbrellas and about the weather, versus what he had before."

Clearly, being in the studio with Jay-Z was anything but predictable. Not only that, but Rihanna's mentor was right behind her. "'Umbrella' was a song that the minute you heard it, you knew what it was going to be – a smash," he claimed. "That's my family right there. We've all been on this journey of Rihanna's growth… it's not just lending my vocals to a project – it's a project and a person I believe in."

Now that they had found what Jay-Z already saw as a chart topper, it was time to record a promotional video. The team enlisted the help of Chris Applebaum, who had worked with her previously on 'S.O.S'. He instantly noticed a change in Rihanna, who was now eager to call the shots in how she was portrayed.

"She couldn't stress enough how much she wanted to take chances," Chris told MTV. "She said, 'Please send me something, but I want to do some choreography. I really want to do some extraordinary performance, but please don't send me anything unless it's really, really out there!' It's probably one of those things that a director is dying to hear from an artist, especially one that I respect and love as much as Rihanna. I knew it was going to be an incredible challenge and that it was going to be really exciting."

It might have been exciting, but it was also nerve-wracking. Now that he knew Rihanna was expecting something groundbreaking from him – only the best – he was under enormous pressure to deliver something the star herself would approve of, not just the record company. It wasn't often that an artist who had started off as a manufactured act grew into demanding creative control. Racing against a tight deadline, she was also demanding urgency – not ideal for a man whose motto was, "I'll send something when it's great, not when it's on time."

Fortunately for him, he had a brainwave, but he wasn't sure that the previously demure and conservative Rihanna would agree to it. It was beyond out there – it involved being totally naked and smothering herself in silver glittery body paint.

Rihanna listened. It wasn't a revolutionary idea. Christina Milian had already coated herself in black body-paint for her video 'Dip It Low', and there was nothing Rihanna hated more than comparisons to other pop artists. That said, what she had in mind was not sizzling sex appeal like Christina – whose body paint had a skin-tight latex look – but an artistic vibe. When she saw things in this context, it instantly reminded her of her idol Grace Jones, a tough and androgynous Jamaican artist who would inspire Lady Gaga among others – and who just so happened to have worn body paint in one of her music videos. The song was her Eighties number 'I'm Not Perfect (But I'm Perfect For You)'.

"I love Grace Jones!" Rihanna confirmed to *The Guardian*. "She's just amazing. The things she did, the things she wore, her fashion, from holding a cigarette to having a flat-top boy haircut. It took a really strong person to do that and as a female, I look at her like, 'You are amazing!' These days a lot of people in the industry wear stuff on stage that they would wear on the street instead of having fun with the fact that you're on stage."

Perhaps it was time for Rihanna to practise what she'd been preaching. After all, Grace was one of her biggest muses and body paint had worked for her. Plus it seemed from Chris's brief that he had the same theme in mind as her.

"I asked her how she would feel if she were a classic Greek statue," he told MTV. "Like, would people find that to be sexy? I wrote the idea thinking that we need to redefine the way in which people have seen this type of body paint and can she become a character within this that isn't her but more of an alter ego?"

Rihanna agreed. Not only was she willing to take more risks and ask for more control than she had done as a shy teenager during the 'S.O.S.' shoot, but she was contributing her own ideas too. Chris was alarmed when she revealed to him that, despite having had no technical training at all, her fantasy was to be a ballerina for the shoot.

"Rihanna asked me, 'Can I go *en pointe*? I feel like I can figure out how to do it and make it work,'" he recalled. "I said, 'OK, can I see it?', and nobody showed it to me until like the day before the shoot, and physically it's really painful because she's on the tips of her toes. There's a way in which you're supporting your entire body just by being on your toes." He added, "I don't think a lot of people can really do it and somehow she learned how to do that and I think that it was really painful for her. But I think she was really determined to make it work and she just went for it."

There were two themes running through the video. The first was of a good girl turning bad, featuring Rihanna dressed all in white to represent the innocent side of herself, and then reverting to black to channel her naughtier side. Throughout, she was twirling with an umbrella which metaphorically offered protection from negativity. In that case, the raindrops she needed protection from were the cruel words of her detractors, which had come strong and fast since she had entered the public eye.

However, the most ambitious scenes – and Rihanna's favourite ones to shoot – took place with the body paint. "It was actually fun doing it because it's probably something that I'll only do once in my lifetime," she told *Men's Fitness*, dashing readers' hopes of a repeat performance. "Two women painted me, spraying coat after coat. Then I stood in a big black box so that no-one could see me in the nude while I filmed. There were only, like, eight people in the box including the director and my manager."

Although Rihanna was about to be screened to the whole world naked, she was unusually coy about those in the room seeing her – particularly Jay-Z, as she felt it would stir up old rumours. As it was, she would later find herself accused of indecency, forcing her to defend herself: "When I did that metallic body paint stuff... I didn't do it to show my body. I didn't do it for people to like me. I did it because it was a cool visual, unexpected and it looked hot." She added, "My mother would kill me if I posed nude!"

Jay-Z also took time out to appear in person and perform his rap in the video. Rihanna was thrilled. "It was absolutely an honour!" she shared with *Concrete Loop.* "People go through their career dreaming of a collaboration with Jay-Z and here I am, my first single on my third album. It was perfect timing, the perfect song to do with him and just being on the video set, it had me tripped out a little because I was like, 'Wow, I'm shooting a video with Jay-Z!' It was crazy."

The video moved several people. While shooting, Chris heard a sobbing sound. Incredulous, he looked down to find his assistant in floods of tears. Concerned, he asked between takes whether she was alright. "She looked at me and said, 'Chris, this is the most incredible thing I've ever seen!'," he recalled. "It really felt like we were shooting something unique at that moment."

However, the magic couldn't last forever and it was back to reality. Within just a few hours, the shoot was over – but the effects of her all-over paintwork would last much longer. A frustrated Rihanna told *Men's Fitness,* "The body paint was really silly. I couldn't wait to get it off my face! That was the worst part about it – getting it off! I was in the shower for two and a half hours!" She added, "My best friend had to come and shower with me, because after I tried to do it myself, the silver would just go back to where I just washed myself. She was just like, 'Take your hands off and let me do it.' Days after, I still had some in my hair, ears, even my belly button. It would not come off."

If the idea of some hands-on contact while bathing with her best friend conjured up lesbian fantasies in the minds of the world's red-blooded men, they were to be bitterly disappointed. Rihanna was at pains to point out that she might be taking risks, but – for now at least – she wasn't as sexually liberated as she seemed. It was purely her artistic output that she had in mind.

"It's very important for me to show people who I am because fans can connect with me more [but] when people see the video, the first thing they say is that I got sexier and I wasn't even thinking about that!" she told *Men's Fitness.* "Everything I wore is a reflection of how I felt, a reflection of where I am right now. And even the part in the video where I'm painted silver, people really talk about that and I wasn't even thinking about being naked, I was looking at the visual. It's more artistic for me – so it's definitely showing people me more rather than trying to look sexy." She added, "It just came naturally. I didn't say, 'I'm going to put this on. It's going to be sexy. It's going to be dark.' I didn't really think about these things."

'Umbrella' debuted in the USA on March 29 and was released to the public in May throughout the rest of the world. It turned out to be more of a chart-topper than even Jay-Z had anticipated, shooting to the number one spot in almost 30 countries. On the US *Billboard* chart, it held that position for seven weeks and in the UK it remained for a mighty ten weeks – the longest running number one in the country since 1994.

The timing, however, was bad. Torrential thunderstorms, severe weather warnings and flash floods swamped the UK almost as soon as the song hit the charts. It was one of the worst summers in most people's lifetimes with, according to statistics, the wettest June since records had begun.

Joking that the freak weather conditions had been created in Rihanna's honour, *The Sun* newspaper described the song as a 'curse' and encouraged readers to kick it off the top spot as soon as they could. The feature read, "Looking back, 'Umbrella' seemed destined to bring bad luck. The video to the track was shot on Friday, April 13. Before the single was released on May 14, Britain had been basking in sunshine. London was Europe's warmest capital along with Athens as temperatures soared to 20°C. But just one day after the song hit the shops... downpours and flash floods devastated the country." Insisting that party-goers might have been unwittingly performing a rain dance, *The Sun* requested that people "knock the song off the top spot for ever, ever, ever" and urged them to "flush 'Umbrella' down the drain where it brolly well belongs!"

While tunes like 'Summertime' by Jazzy Jeff and the Fresh Prince or 'Sunny Afternoon' by The Kinks no doubt all received a download boost, Rihanna's position remained unchanged. The nation might have joked about the "curse of Rihanna's umbrella", but her chart ranking stayed stable and the song remained at number one for a further week.

When *OMM* asked Rihanna to offer an apology for the weather, she laughed, "People were grilling me about it, and I was like, 'What? It's a coincidence!' But actually, I think it was the other way round, the bad weather helped my song stay on top!"

She added to Q magazine, "The weather definitely helped the song stay there for so long. People hate the rain, but here was this song that speaks about the rain and makes you feel great – even if the weather is horrible!"

Whatever the critics thought, the song was a record breaker. It became the bestseller of 2007 worldwide, selling nine million singles. Rihanna had also been successfully holding Beyoncé and Shakira's 'Beautiful Liar' off the top spot. Even more importantly, it had the biggest debut on the download chart since iTunes began – a record previously held by Shakira and Wyclef Jean with 'Hips Don't Lie'. That was significant for Rihanna because it was 'Hips Don't Lie' that had earned three times more votes than 'S.O.S.' in the Viewer's Choice category of the 2006 Video Music Awards. It had also been a barrier between her and the number one position when she first began in the industry. She had battled against it when 'Pon De Replay' was released, so it was immensely satisfying to rise above the artists who had once conquered her.

However, the biggest achievement for her was breaking records in the UK. "It's number one there off digital downloads only," she had enthused to *Concrete Loop* at the time, "which has never been done by a female artist before. So I made history there and it astounded me... this is definitely going to be the highlight of my career."

In the midst of her total domination of the singles charts, the new album was released on May 30, 2007. Photographer Roberto D'Este had masterminded the visual side of her transformation from good girl to bad, taking the pictures that had appeared on the album sleeve. Cover photos are all-important in building an image that fans can relate to and, fearing confusion at the sudden change, Rihanna's management had wanted to take things slowly.

"In agreement with Def Jam and her team, we just wanted to make her fresh and not to push the envelope too much," Roberto told the author. "She was only 19 and we thought it would have been important to gradually build her image without skipping steps."

But an "extremely confident" Rihanna had other ideas, wanting to take a leading role in how she should look. "There was a lot of input from her, especially about styling and hair. She brought a lot of tear sheets to the meetings and, for a young girl, she had quite a clear idea of what she wanted," he recalled. "She wanted it sexy, not vulgar."

For the first time, Rihanna was enjoying her photo shoots. They were no longer generic beach scenes where her look was pre-planned to the last detail. She came to life; but, because of her youth, her ideas needed fine-tuning. "She would jump from one idea to another, and at times it didn't work," Roberto said. "Continuity was important, but she had too many ideas so we had to channel them to our purposes."

However, they got there in the end. "It was definitely a more aggressive look," he added approvingly. "She seemed more confident. She made that step from girl to woman."

Sound-wise, the album achieved some rave reviews, with *AllMusic* claiming it was "as pop as pop gets" and that, just as she had hoped for when she was channelling Brandy, "each one of its 12 songs [is] a potential hit." The *New York Times* added to the praise, saying, "This CD sounds as if it was scientifically engineered to deliver hits."

Rihanna's fanbase began to expand, too. She made the number one spot in Japan, Russia and Brazil with the album – territories that had previously barely heard of her. It also made number one in the UK, Ireland and Canada and number two in the USA and Australia.

However, some criticised the release, claiming it was still heavily manufactured and lacked authenticity. For instance, Rihanna had told one interviewer that men who were overconfident repelled her, claiming, "If a guy is arrogant – if he's hot and he knows it – forget it!" Yet on 'Push Up On Me', someone who is extremely confident is the perfect man. To some, it didn't feel as though she believed her own lyrics.

Similarly in 'Question Existing', fans had thought Rihanna was opening her heart about something deeply personal during her diary-style confessional, only to discover that it wasn't her who had written the lyrics. Rihanna had to explain that she relied on Ne-Yo to say "exactly what I feel."

While the perils of fame was clearly a subject that the two of them had in common, there were critics who felt she ought to have had more personal input in order to truly live her lyrics. Moreover, even in the light-hearted 'Lemme Get That', Rihanna had revealed she was simply playing a character.

Fans were keen to get to know the real Rihanna, the one that she had promised in the media when she talked about her image overhaul. So far, the self-expression in her look wasn't transferring so consistently to the sound. Rihanna defended her decision not to co-write any of the tracks on her biggest selling album so far, telling *Entertainment Weekly*, "I love song writing, but if the song is great, I just leave it. I'm not one of those people who's like, 'I have to have a publishing credit!' It's not about that – it's about making great music."

The album was also criticised by none other than Amy Winehouse. Although Rihanna had been talking about her love for the reckless soul singer, telling *Star Pulse,* "I want her to get better… it'd be awesome to go on tour with her in the States," it seemed that her love wasn't quite reciprocated. Amy objected to the use of the song title 'Rehab', which she implied was a copy of her own. "Rihanna, you owe me!" she raged on her Twitter account.

Amy's direct approach didn't spare Rihanna's blushes, but attention was soon diverted away from the playful feud when Rihanna's next single, 'Shut Up And Drive', hit the charts. The video, shot in a Prague junkyard, saw Rihanna posing beside a Ferrari. In the background are broken-up cars destined to be junked, and pieces of scrap metal, while Rihanna's ride stands out as looking impeccable. Perhaps it was a metaphor for how she had risen above the other artists in the music world by being different. Plus, while jazz and R&B vocalist Natalie Cole had sung of a 'Pink Cadillac' in the Eighties, Rihanna wasn't about to be so feminine – hers was sleek and black. What's more, her black leather jacket and dominant demeanour are seen to intimidate men at the garage as she leans into their car window, further cementing her fearless persona.

The website *About.com* praised the video: "Like any successful sports car, the look, feel and speed of 'Shut Up And Drive' pull you in, despite the model's shortcomings." It also reflected on Rihanna's rush to the top, marvelling, "Rihanna has established herself as the most consistent pop hit maker of the moment." She was under some pressure to deliver, with *BBC News* adding expectantly that, while 'Umbrella' was Rihanna's biggest hit to date, there was "plenty on the album that could do even better". No longer a special interest artist tucked away in the corner of the CD store, away from the big hits, Rihanna had now become a pop sensation – and expectations were high.

When the single hit the shops on June 12, it didn't disappoint. While it only made it to number three in the US, it peaked at number one in several other countries, including the UK.

It was followed by 'Hate That I Love You', which came with a headline-drawing video featuring Ne-Yo. The two are presented as ex-lovers with a special bond. Both end up with other people, but neither can keep the other off their mind. When they meet in an elevator, Rihanna gives him a sad smile, knowing he will always be on the honours list in her heart – before climbing into a car with her new beau.

The song, released on August 21, implies an addictive relationship that both will use as a measure for the rest of their lives. MSN favoured the fact that it didn't seem to be another cheesy love story, commenting that the video tells "a familiar tale in a refreshingly unclichéd manner". It didn't match the success of the first two singles, however, earning a number seven spot in the USA and a comparatively measly number 15 spot in the UK, but she did earn a record total of more than 67 million views on YouTube.

Life had become crazy for Rihanna and it was about to get crazier. That year, although jokey rumours and idle gossip circulated about stars insuring their body parts, including claims that Jennifer Lopez had insured her famously curvaceous bottom for a six-figure sum, Rihanna really had taken such a step. Her legs had been insured for $1 million by razor brand Venus Breeze as part of her sponsorship deal with them.

Just two years earlier, she had been an unknown school girl who hadn't even finished her high-school exams. She had been working more than 11 hours a day in the music business with no guarantee of success. Life had been difficult. She had been overwhelmed by the culture shock of moving to America for the first time, adjusting to the bitterly cold east-coast climate. No doubt she would have used an umbrella for the very first time to shield her from the rain – and now she was hurtling around the world's video screens with what had once been an unknown object. Ludicrously, she even had her own range of five different types of Rihanna umbrellas in her merchandise line. She had also been elevated to a status which entitled her to make diva-like demands. While Rihanna was adamant that she didn't play that card often, insuring her legs was the first step on the road to extravagant divadom. Even if she kept the card hidden, she had it safely in her deck.

Most importantly of all, she had finally found the freedom to express herself. "At first I just took what was given to me," she reflected to *The Observer*, "but eventually I started saying, 'No.' I said, 'I don't want to wear that and I want to wear my hair like this.' Now I'm in complete control of my image and everything else. It takes time. You learn."

Rihanna dresses all in black but for the bright pink umbrella as she performs one of the first of many renditions of hit single 'Umbrella'. JEFF KRAVITZ/FILM MAGIC

In a neon pink floor-length gown, Rihanna poses with Chris Applebaum, the director who persuaded her to strip naked and douse herself in gold paint for the video of 'Umbrella'. They were at the MTV Video Music Awards at Las Vegas's Palms Hotel on September 9, 2007. ETHAN MILLER/GETTY IMAGES

Rebel without a cause: Rihanna perfects her best intense and moody expression as she begs someone to help her in a 2007 rendition of 'SOS' at the Legacy Recording Studios in New York. ROBERT SABO/NY DAILY NEWS ARCHIVE VIA GETTY IMAGES

Rihanna and Ne-Yo delight a Los Angeles audience with a duet at the Nokia Theatre to mark the 2007 American Music Awards on November 18, 2007 ETHAN MILLER/GETTY IMAGES

For some it's fetish wear, but for Rihanna S&M chic is all in an ordinary day's work – here she rocks the leather look with some patent thigh-high boots for an October 11, 2007 concert at New York's Nokia Theatre

JAMIE McCARTHY/WIREIMAGE

Rihanna attends the Grammy Awards in LA on February 10, 2008, accepting a win for the Best Rap/Sung Collaboration for 'Umbrella'. VINCE BUCCI/GETTY IMAGES

A perfectly poised Rihanna stands tall next to her more diminutive singing partners Beyonce and Miley Cyrus at New York's Fashion Rocks event on September 5, 2008. (KEVIN MAZUR/WIREIMAGE)

Gangsta Chic: Rihanna dons a cropped leather jacket and dark sunglasses, coming across as cold as ice for a performance with T.I at the MTV Video Music Awards in LA on September 7, 2008. KEVIN WINTER/GETTY IMAGES

Turning up the temperature: Rihanna heats up a cold December night for the audience at the 2008 Z100 Jingle Ball at New York's Madison Square Garden as she and Chris Brown seductively serenade one another on the stage. KEVIN MAZUR/WIREIMAGE FOR CLEAR CHANNEL ENTERTAINMENT

Chapter 5

Every Rose Has Its Thorn

Rihanna's life seemed near perfect – but for how much longer? This year, 2007, was the year that Amy Winehouse had a life-threatening seizure and – reluctantly – said 'Yes, yes, yes' to rehab. It was the year that party girl Paris Hilton had been imprisoned for driving offences and photographed in floods of tears in a patrol car. Britney Spears had shaved her head and almost lost custody of her children, and Kate Moss had shown the nation just how she earned the nickname 'Cocaine Kate'. Meanwhile US reality TV star Kim Kardashian was cringing in embarrassment after a graphic sex tape was released featuring her in the lead role.

In 2007, if you were a young female celebrity, a rock'n'roll drama seemed almost obligatory. Whether it was crack smoking on camera, tales of teenage heroin addiction or crumbling septums (destroyed by cocaine abuse) plunging down plug-holes, every performer seemed to have a story to tell. It seemed that money, fame and success went hand in hand with public meltdowns of epic proportions. However, so far, Rihanna seemed to have escaped most of the pitfalls of fame. Cool, calm and serene, she wasn't far off being a role model. Yet every rose has its thorn, as she was about to find out.

In September, she was still riding on the wave of the success of 'Umbrella' when she and fellow R&B star Chris Brown performed together at the MTV Video Music Awards. Thousands watched the pair's medley of hits, including 'Umbrella' and Michael Jackson's 'Billie Jean', at the September 9 ceremony in the luxurious Palms hotel in Las Vegas. That night she won awards for Video of the Year and Monster Single of the Year. Rihanna was elated.

Yet, barely over a week later, the mood had changed dramatically. What was more, as she embarked on her biggest tour yet, there was nowhere to hide from the harsh glare of the media spotlight. On September 20, she received a review of a show in Vancouver with the humiliating headline, "Akon shows Rihanna how it's done." The feature implied that she was in her support act's shadow, sneering, "The kindest thing you can say about Rihanna is that she's shown some improvement since her last visit. For a start, she no longer seems tone deaf."

It went on to dismiss her cover of her idol Bob Marley's 'Is This Love?' as "tuneless mangling" and her rendition of 'Pon De Replay' as "drum and bass in a garbage can". Rihanna, who had been proud of learning ballet steps in a matter of days for the 'Umbrella' video shoot, now found herself described as an amateur who "couldn't outdance" the one-legged Heather Mills. The review concluded that she had "plenty to learn about keeping an audience engaged", a talent which it recommended she gleaned from Akon.

Subsequent reviews spoke of lacklustre, robotic performances, and the list of critics Rihanna could apply the lyrics of 'Question Existing' to was growing by the day. Although it was customary in Barbados to keep personal problems behind closed doors, something was very obviously wrong. She finally revealed to *The Sunday Times* that she was feeling cripplingly lonely.

"At first, I was on an adrenalin high – this is my dream, I'm actually doing it. It didn't faze me that I was alone, that I wasn't with the people I love," she said. "But after a while, it got repetitive and that's when you kind of go, 'Oh wow, I'm sitting in a hotel room once again, me and the television.' When you're in the spotlight, people are like, 'What do you have to worry about?' They forget that the success is one great aspect of your life, but behind that there are problems, there are dark sides, there's loneliness, unhappiness."

That unseasonably cold autumn, the sun truly had gone out for Rihanna – in more ways than one. The more people that adored her, the less confident she felt. She loved being on stage – after all, "when you're in the spotlight, everything seems good." Yet after every show, the elation of fans screaming her name faded, until she was just Robyn again – a lonely, conflicted woman who doubted the adulation and doubted herself.

"I did a show in Belgrade," she continued. "We were expecting 6,000 people and 24,000 showed up. And I didn't understand why. I look at them and I still think, 'Why are you screaming for me?' I still think of myself as a normal girl."

Overwhelmed with emotion, for the first time ever in an interview she began to cry. She called herself an ordinary teenager – albeit someone who had just insured their legs for a princely sum – and, true to that description, she lacked the self-worth to believe she deserved all the adulation. If anything, it made her more confused and more unhappy. According to *The Sunday Times*, multi-million-selling albums and unprecedented success were yet to provide her with "meaningful, as opposed to superficial, affirmation of her real worth". The interviewer added, "Behind her, she has guiding hands on her shoulders; in front exploding flash-bulbs and inquisitive fans. Neither seems especially comforting."

Even less comforting were Rihanna's equally traumatic red-carpet experiences. "Everybody's calling your name," she recalled. "That was weird to me. And I thought I wasn't pleasing them. They all sounded so angry. 'Rihanna, look here.' 'No, look here, Rihanna.'"

Plus, being on the road wasn't always about the ease of helicopters and first-class travel. Sometimes it involved cramped coaches and rickety tour buses. Journeys could be long and distances prohibitive. If it wasn't the isolation of another anonymous hotel room – where she had thousands of fans, but no real friends – it was the all-night journeys on her tour bus. Far from a glamorous existence, the opportunity to travel the world and see a new city every morning meant that she wasn't able to stay in the same place for long enough to make friends or put down roots. She was living her dream, but she was doing it alone. Craving someone to share it with, Rihanna flew over friends from Barbados whenever she could, but they had their own lives. One was a medical student while another was working flat-out studying law and economics. A couple more had children back in Bridgetown and had too many commitments to join her on tour.

The long hours and lack of friends eventually began to take their toll on Rihanna and some of her concerts failed to live up to expectations. On her British tour, three shows were cancelled altogether due to health problems. It was something that critics weren't about to let her forget. Some reviewers even scolded her for the 'workhorse ethic' that had led to her illness.

In Belfast, complete with thigh-high PVC boots and a barely-there black leather bondage outfit, Rihanna was fulfilling her promise to deliver sizzling sex appeal. *The Mirror* reported that she looked as though she had "stepped out of a sex shop" and that "her boobs seemed to be four times bigger" than her outfit. However, that wasn't enough for an increasingly demanding and unforgiving team of critics.

By the time the tour reached Wembley Arena in London on December 16, Rihanna was entering public career meltdown. She was suffering from burn-out, exhaustion and depression, which reviewers interpreted as boredom. According to *The Daily Mail*, her performance was "strikingly cold and controlled". And while the whole world seemed mesmerised by Rihanna's new look, when she had to get on stage and show the goods, not everyone was as impressed. In fact, the same reviewer dismissed her appearance as "curiously unerotic" and her onstage seduction technique as merely "mechanical".

When she took to the stage an hour late due to an unexplained technical issue, *The Times* scolded, "Perhaps the Barbadian singer feels that she has earned the right to behave like a diva. The album is, after all, called *Good Girl Gone Bad*. Or perhaps she feels she is simply being worked too hard. Either way, she remained regally unapologetic when she finally did arrive." While the reviewer acknowledged that Rihanna thanked fans for "being so patient", offered declarations of love for them and told them that London was her favourite city in the world on numerous occasions, she remained unsympathetic to the singer, claiming, "She delivered these lines with a robotic lack of sincerity… Although frequently compared to Beyoncé, Rihanna was not in the same league, either as a singer or a personality."

An exhausted Rihanna was being demotivated – both due to her tiredness and the disappointment of the multiple bad reviews. This in turn seemed to lead to a vicious circle of even more bad reviews. "What's missing is any flicker of spontaneity," the *Daily Mail* insisted. "She can't fake it and looks awkward trying. When she declares 'I'm having so much fun,' she sounds as if she's reading a cue card."

No-one in the media seemed to understand her plight. One headline screamed, "Self-pitying Rihanna sings of the harsh life of the over-pampered pop princess." It went on to attribute the success of her album to the guest appearances of already established stars and warned darkly, "Without more hits, this reign will soon pass."

Most reviews of the Wembley show were wholly negative, with the exception of *The Guardian*, who gave her act five stars. The paper felt that, underneath her edgy image and sexy clothes and the act of maturity, there was a vulnerable young girl going through the biggest changes of her life, and in far greater agony than her detractors gave her credit for. "With three albums already under her belt, it's easy to forget that Rihanna is still a teenager, all of 19," it claimed. "Unlike most teenage pop stars, she has rarely traded on her youth and only the occasional touch of endearingly wide-eyed sincerity betrays her age… Rihanna takes to the big-budget spectacle as if she were born for it."

But, although she had just landed a private show for the Russian oligarch Roman Abramovich, which would net her a reported £300,000, Rihanna was desperately unhappy and overworked, and she couldn't wait to get home. "I miss so much," she told *US* magazine. "I miss home. I miss The Boatyard – that's my favourite club. I miss my friends. I miss my two younger brothers. I miss the beach and the food."

She didn't have to wait long to cure her teenage homesickness. She was due a few days off for Christmas and she would be jetting back to spend the festive season with family. However, even back home there was no respite from the bad press. The people of Barbados were not as universally welcoming as the nation's biggest female star might have hoped for. One of their biggest gripes was her sexy image. In spite of that, Rihanna was adamant that she reserved the raunchiest items for the stage. "My street wear is very respectful," she told *The Mirror*. "It's cool, casual, a little sexy but not overly so because that stuff is for the stage."

She had recently turned down a lucrative offer from *FHM Germany* to pose topless, but in Barbados she was still seen as immodest. A swimsuit she wore on the beach that year made headline news; it was emblazoned across the front page of newspapers and inspired furious letters from conservative parents. Rihanna believed the photographer had deliberately insinuated that she was wearing her swimwear in the street.

"I had on a one-piece swimsuit with jeans, but the swimsuit obviously, it had the back out and stuff, the sides out," Rihanna explained. "They took the picture and they made it look like it was a top that was really revealing. There were call-in radio programmes about it. It was a big deal for, like, three weeks straight – talking about how I'm not setting a good example."

The news was a huge blow. Not only had she hoped for a few days out of the spotlight, surrounded by supportive people, but she worried that the swimsuit affair had put her public image in crisis.

She was no longer just a normal girl – instead, she found her every move being scrutinised. The eyes of a nation were on her, children included, and every action she took carried the weight of responsibility. While her stage show featured dominatrix-style latex, spike heels and dancers with whips –and was a part of what had made Rihanna a visual icon – she was reluctant to be seen as someone who played on their sex appeal to gain fans.

"I don't like to wear things that are too skimpy," she defended. "If I do shorts on the bottom, it's got to be something very conservative at the top. If it's skimpy at the top, it's got to be long jeans or something. I like to balance it out. I won't do short shorts and short top." She added, "That's what I admire so much about Alicia Keys. She became so successful off of just her music. She was really conservative about her style at first."

Rihanna had chosen to play the role of bad girl – and now she feared she would suffer the consequences. But, unexpectedly, she also found herself at the centre of another race debate, both in the US and in Barbados – something she thought she had left behind in her schooldays.

Nearly nine million readers had cast votes for *FHM* USA's 100 Sexiest Women poll. When the results came in, just four women of black origin were featured on the list. What was more, all of them were mixed race, with much lighter skin than a conventional black girl. The women chosen were Beyoncé, the actresses Selita Ebanks and Halle Berry – and, of course, Rihanna herself.

Understandably, some reactions in the black community were of crushing disappointment. One girl asked, on web forum *Gossip Rocks*, "The question I have is, why all of the 'hot black chicks' in the industry are mixed race, or at least multi-racial with obvious European features? Look at the black women mentioned in this poll. Why can't a 100% black chick be considered hot?"

Another concurred. "It seems that even in the black community, there is this huge issue of colourism, where the mixed-race, lighter skinned women are considered hotter." Another woman suggested, "I think it's a reflection of the industry in general, the fact that 99% of the women in the showbiz industry are white."

Although black women were still a minority group in North America compared to those of white origin, the results of the poll nevertheless raised the awkward question of why more black women were not chosen to be actresses or singers, and why many of those that did make the grade were rarely featured in the public eye.

To some infuriated onlookers, women of colour were deliberately marginalised and, when they were seen, it seemed only to be as a token gesture. Inevitably, when the news hit Barbados, anger turned towards Rihanna. Those who had flooded message forums on the internet when she had first got signed, with comments that Jay-Z had chosen her for her pale skin, went back on the offensive.

Accused of being too sexy, too white and too provocative, Rihanna wasn't feeling very popular in Barbados. It was rumoured that, when she finally left the island to return to America, it wasn't without shedding a few tears.

Yet, as lonely as she felt, her professional life only continued to accelerate. 'Don't Stop The Music', accompanied by the first video Rihanna had a role in directing, was climbing the charts with a Top 10 spot in 25 countries, while 'Umbrella' was even earning kudos in the rock world. The Manic Street Preachers, a group with a notorious hatred for 'bubblegum pop' and 'mainstream chart music', had warmed to the song so much that they had recorded their own version. Bassist Nicky Wire told the *NME*, "This was my favourite track of 2007. It's just so razor-sharp. And who'd have thought a song called 'Umbrella' would be number one all over the world? It's just such an un-pop word. I love it when a record seems to come from another universe!"

Meanwhile, at the 2008 Brit Awards, the Klaxons mixed it with their own song 'Golden Skans' for a live rendition that Rihanna loved. She told *BBC 6 Music*, "It was really different, very cool, unexpected. But when I hear it, I just want to hear it more. It makes it so much more rock'n'roll." She added that she had been inspired to record a new version just like it.

Meanwhile, Madonna was organising a charity fundraiser in partnership with Gucci to benefit both UNICEF and her own charity, Raising Malawi, and Rihanna was billed to be a part of it. For Madonna's part, her love affair with Malawi had begun in 2006 when she had founded her charity in honour of the nation's one million AIDS orphans.

The country was poverty-stricken and disease-infested, and its children were under-educated and desperately malnourished. In a bid to help, Madonna adopted a child – a decision which she was widely criticised for in the press – and vowed to channel as much money as possible into the cause, both through her own donations and by using her celebrity status and cash to raise awareness. (She would later be engulfed in scandal when some £2.4 million, donated to build a school, was spent on staff perks, without a single brick having been laid.)

The fundraiser itself, A Night To Benefit Raising Malawi and UNICEF – which was held in New York on February 6, 2008, to mark the opening of a new Gucci store – also created controversy. Both Madonna and Gucci were accused of using the cause to raise their own public profiles, to build up a humanitarian image to boost sales via the free publicity. Some said it was exploitative and patronising, but the guest list – which read like a 'Who's Who' of Hollywood – was filled with people who seemed to think otherwise.

Gwyneth Paltrow, Gwen Stefani, Tom Cruise, Dita von Teese and a heavily pregnant Jennifer Lopez were all in attendance. "When Madonna asks you to do something, you do it," fashion designer Matthew Williamson said by way of explanation. While it might have seemed that Madonna had half of Hollywood under hypnosis to obey her orders, it was all for a good cause – and by auctioning off celebrity events, such as aerobics sessions with Madonna, more than $5 million was raised. Performers at the event included Timbaland and Alicia Keys – and of course Rihanna, who would later be inspired to host her own charity events. "It's a great honour to me to able to use my celebrity for a worthy cause," she claimed.

It was a special few days for Rihanna since, on February 10, she earned her very first Grammy. Not only that, but she had a close friend by her side – LA-based R&B star Chris Brown. A teenage sensation one year her junior, he had already been described as the next Michael Jackson and had been discovered almost by accident, by talent scouts who happened to pop into his father's petrol station.

Both he and Rihanna were signed to Island Def Jam within months of each other, and both released their debut albums in 2005. Initially, Chris was more successful than Rihanna, becoming the first male artist to have a debut single top the US charts since 1995. And while she was under pressure to repeat the success of 'Pon De Replay', enduring dismissive reviews that referred to it as a "one-hit wonder" and "a nice late-summer track, but certainly not something to build a career on", Chris's self-titled album quickly climbed to the top of the charts, selling more than two million copies in the USA alone in a very short space of time. Music critics raved that his dancing might have been better than Michael Jackson's.

He and Rihanna were both building successful careers at the same time and their paths often crossed. However, there were some major differences between the two. While Rihanna was marketed as an innocent girl at the start, Chris's demeanour was very different. One of the key factors in Chris's appeal was marketable misbehaviour –

something the hip-hop world coveted. "I write about things that 16 year olds go through every day," he had told MTV. "Like, you just got in trouble for sneaking your girl into the house, or you can't drive, so you steal a car or something."

His reputation as a bad boy was sealed from the beginning, but that was just the type of man that Rihanna liked – and the two soon built up a firm friendship. That night at the Grammys, he was to share in her success as, together with Jay-Z, she won the award for Best Rap/Sung Collaboration. The night might have belonged to Kanye West, whose four gongs were the talk of the after party, but for Rihanna – who had been nominated in six categories – being remembered for 'Umbrella' was enough. She accepted the award alongside Jay-Z.

In spite of her frosty reception back in Barbados, her peace offering was to dedicate the award to her people. "Barbados, we got one!" she grinned. "I love you!"

Barbados reciprocated the compliment by quickly organising a festival in her honour – Rihanna Day, set to be on February 21. Jetting in by boat to celebrate, Rihanna flaunted her superstar status by arriving with an entourage of policemen, security and aides. She gave a regal wave before being embraced by the island's prime minister, David Thompson, and wished well by hundreds of fans, who clutched bright yellow umbrellas as a gesture of allegiance. Local companies sponsored her with gifts of a Land Rover and a multi-thousand dollar diamond bracelet. The government also offered a free plot of land.

These material gestures might have meant nothing to someone who now had multi-million selling songs topping every chart, but what mattered to her the most was that they were gifts from her people. It could also be a chance to repair the fraught relationship that she had had with the island in recent times.

A delighted Rihanna, who performed for free at her party that night, told the crowd, "I am so grateful and I have never been more proud to be Bajan! I want to thank all of you for coming out and supporting me tonight and my career from day one!"

The following day, Rihanna travelled to Jamaica where she was scheduled to perform as part of the Africa Unite annual concert in celebration of Bob Marley. Many Marley family members would be performing as well as the renowned John Legend, so Rihanna would be in acclaimed company.

The location was James Bond Beach, a stretch of coastline so named because Ian Fleming, the creator of the famous character, had made his home there. Meanwhile, the theme of the concert would be to encourage unity in the black community. A prior youth symposium had dealt with issues affecting Africa such as HIV and AIDS, black leadership and the "role and importance of the girl child".

However, by February 23, the audience had only music on their minds. When Rihanna made her grand entrance at the concert, many were wondering how she would compare to a line-up of what onlookers admiringly branded "professional reggae legends". Would her brand of mainstream pop be sneered at? Would she be belittled for abandoning her roots?

Whatever the answer was, she needn't have worried about being ignored. Her outfit caused a stir, when her ethnic beaded dress revealed an amount of cleavage that would have made glamour model Jordan look prudish in comparison. She was allegedly showing off a brand new boob job, but the crowd called her look "immodest" and "cheap", urging her to "wear your size!"

She attracted endless attention at the event, but it was not just her breast implants, poking through her perilously low cut dress, that fixed all eyes on her. Neither was it her tribute to Jamaica's most famous legend with a four-song set some audience members described as "sensational". Instead, what was really raising eyebrows was Rihanna's appearance with Chris Brown.

He made an unofficial appearance during Elephant Man's set and, according to *Yard Flex*, "almost stole the show". The website reported, "His snake-like movement while dancing and his shrilling voice could not have failed." Humiliatingly for Rihanna, it was claimed that he overshadowed her, in spite of not formally being part of the billing. "She performed as if she did not belong," the website continued. "Her set was lethargic and patrons breathed a sigh of relief when she left the stage."

Not only that, but both the Americans and British newspapers got hold of the story and wrongly reported that Rihanna and Chris had been on holiday together, when in fact her business in Jamaica was the concert. Media speculation about the two had begun around the time of the Grammy Awards, when they were photographed together beside fellow showbiz couple Nas and Kelis, and it had increased even further when paparazzi had snapped them canoodling at a hotel pool in Jamaica.

Ironically, Rihanna had been regularly performing 'Is This Love?' by Bob Marley at her live shows, which was exactly the question the media had begun to ask. Was it a casual fling or a full-blown relationship? According to Rihanna, it was neither. "I won't say that we're just friends," she began teasingly. "Me and Chris are really best, best friends. We both started our careers at the same time. He is one of the only people in the industry I trust and hang out with all the time. We are best friends, honestly, like brother and sister. If he was a boyfriend, I would say that."

Chris seemed equally incredulous about the rumours, insisting, "Me personally, from a relationship standpoint, I am a single guy. I am definitely single. And I've been on my website and seen how girls have been threatening me and saying I'm a liar, and I'm like, 'It's not even that.'" He added to MTV, "I have a close friend, but it's not like a relationship. I'm not trying to settle down. I'm only 18, so I'm just trying to live my life and have fun."

In spite of the pair's denials, they were regularly photographed getting intimate with each other and, before long, the pair had matching tattoos on their necks in the shape of three stars. Could it be that, like Jay-Z and Beyoncé in their early days, they were shrouding their relationship in secrecy to protect themselves from rumours? If so, their silence only added to the feverish speculation.

Chris's manager, Tina Davis, let the cat out of the bag when she revealed that the couple had been dating for a long time and, far from a casual friendship, they were so serious about each other than they would resist separation and pine when they had to be apart. "He adored her," she explained. "It got to the point where they didn't want to be separated. Both we and her management would be saying, 'OK, now you need to go and do this or that,' and they'd reply, 'But we don't want to be apart.' We were like, 'My God, please! Just for five minutes!' We ended up trying to coordinate schedules so that they could both be in the same city at the same time. They loved each other so much."

Yet all the while, the two were playing down suggestions that they had so much as spent the night together. Since the start of her career, Rihanna had admitted to lusting after eligible bachelors in the film and music world – but had insisted that she had no time for a real relationship, that love was "in the background".

However, photographer Roberto D'Este exclusively revealed to the author that their love affair had, in fact, dated as far back as the days when she was fighting to get 'Umbrella' on her album, due to the special meaning it had for her. "In the song, the umbrella represented her boyfriend shading her from everyday problems and troubles," he said. "It was a love song at the end."

Allegedly, those close to the pair feared their relationship was so self-consuming that it would become self-destructive, likening them to Amy Winehouse and her then-husband Blake Fielder-Civil. The same year, Amy had been a no show for her own video shoot, 'Love Is A Losing Game', which many blamed on her relationship. While her manager had been frantically calling her, keeping an entire production crew on standby from 8 a.m. until late evening, the shoot had to be abandoned at a cost of £20,000. When Amy finally made contact, she revealed she had been at home with her husband all the time. She had also made headlines when she began screaming hysterically, sobbing and trying to jump over the Eurostar security gates because she had had a change of heart about leaving her husband behind for just 24 hours. The pair couldn't stand to say goodbye and Amy began to frequently cancel public appearances to be with him.

After her marriage, Amy had seemed to transform overnight from an ambitious career woman who loved nothing more than to perform to an insecure wreck who claimed that she was "not put here [on earth] to sing, but to be a wife". Having seen the celebrity meltdowns that stardom seemed to invite, those in Rihanna's circle were anxious in case she met the same fate. Some felt Rihanna and Chris were dangerously dependent on each other, although they lacked the backdrop of drugs and self-harm that had blighted Amy and Blake.

Although it was an obsessive relationship, and Chris was notorious for his bad boy image, the ultra-protective Jay-Z, who was a father figure to Rihanna, seemed to have accepted it. According to her, those who didn't meet with his approval weren't allowed into her world.

What was more, instead of simply whispering sweet nothings and avoiding work, the two had quickly built up a partnership in the studio too. They wrote 'Bad Girl' together, a song about a compulsive shopaholic with a penchant for Cavalli, Gucci, Louis Vuitton and Versace. The girl in the song is addicted to buying high-fashion clothes and, although the character isn't famous, her wardrobe is so extensive that it has attracted its very own groupies. However, as she doesn't have a bottomless wallet, she defines her excesses as a problem.

Another track the pair worked on was 'Electric Guitar', a duet between the two that was intended to appear on Chris's next album. In the song, music reminds Rihanna of her lover. Every strum of the guitar strings provokes intense emotion, as she claims that it destroys her to be apart from him. Chris asks her to control him with her melody, a request Rihanna eagerly responds to. An early version of the song, recorded without Rihanna's vocals, was leaked onto the internet, infuriating Chris. "I'm mad that it's leaked," he told *The Associated Press*. "The record's not finished yet. It's supposed to be me and Rihanna's duet."

In spite of these setbacks, it seemed that the two had been inspiring each other creatively – and according to Chris's producer, Polow da Don, Rihanna was a joy to work with. "It's easy because Chris Brown's energy alone is incredible," he told MTV. "He's a high-energy kid. Rihanna has a unique voice – she's one of the easiest people to work with."

Although Rihanna was not as yet experienced enough to take a leading role in the writing process, he revealed that she was willing to contribute ideas. "When her, Chris and myself are in the room, it's fun," he continued. "That's when the music isn't work at all – it's freestyle. Chris comes up with an idea, I come up with one [and] Rihanna will weigh in. And we build."

Being desperately in love hadn't stopped Rihanna from getting involved in charity, either. She began to build the Believe Foundation, which she had started in late 2006 to fulfil her childhood dream of changing the world for the better. Children had always been her soft spot due to mothering her brothers from such an early age, and in her pre-teen years she had been extremely affected by documentaries she had watched on kids suffering from cancer. Her dream of helping had come true, as she was now publicly working to raise awareness of blood cancers and petitioning for bone marrow transplant donors to aid the victims of such illnesses. While she focused on children, whose young lives she hated to see shortened when they had barely begun, her campaign was for people of all ages. Rihanna organised three charity concerts in March and April, hitting Chicago, San Francisco and New York. The Bear Necessities Pediatric Cancer Foundation would receive a donation for each show.

At around the same time, Rihanna was alarmed to hear of a mother with leukaemia, Lisa Gershowitz-Flynn, who faced certain death if a donor was not found within six weeks. The clock was ticking – and things were not looking good in her quest for a compatible match.

Fearing for the welfare of Lisa's children if they lost their mother, Rihanna launched a campaign to help. "Lisa is a mother of two… and she was going to die if she didn't get a bone-marrow transplant. I knew she could not leave her two kids," she told *Glamour*. "That's all that was going through my head. So we said a lot of prayers."

That wasn't all she was doing. Her campaign, together with the international donor network DKMS, was a success. "We actually recruited and registered roughly 2,000 new donors, just from phone calls and emails we got," claimed DKMS's vice president Katherina Harf. Despite the brief time available to save Lisa's life, a donor was found. Lisa sent out a public email of gratitude, insisting, "The English language does not have words that are adequate to thank someone for working to save your life… for Rihanna to even be thinking about helping others and putting herself out there when she is so busy with her career is tremendous."

Rihanna told *People* magazine, "My own charity, Believe, works specifically with children in need. Children need their mothers more than anything else in the world. Lisa has two children. My charity will continue to work for DKMS, because in finding a way to save Lisa's life, we will in turn be saving her children's lives."

As someone who had endured a wounding childhood herself, regularly feeling fear, sadness and insecurity, Rihanna had a special infinity with troubled children. The three charity shows she had organised gave her an opportunity to meet some, sign autographs for them and treat them to a front-row position at one of her concerts. The shows revealed a gentler side to Rihanna, whose performances were temporarily free from leather whips and gyrating hips. The children loved it.

"When I was young and I would watch television and I would see all the children suffering, I always said, 'When I grow up, I want to help!'" Rihanna explained at her Chicago show. "Not long after, I was in the position where I could help... as a kid, the one thing I hated most was disappointment, so I never want to disappoint kids. I always want to put a smile on their faces. Kids are the future."

Despite her efforts, Rihanna found herself heavily criticised in Barbados by people who believed that charity started at home and that she wasn't doing enough on a grass-roots level to honour the country who raised her. While glossy celebrity magazines such as *People* were running stories praising her kindness, back home *The Nation News* demanded to know why she was not doing the same – if not more – for Barbados.

Responding to outrage from some Barbadians who had heard showbiz gossip about Rihanna holding parties for her new-found celebrity friends, columnist Carol Martindale published a full-page story on the debate. "Rihanna needs to look into... finding some way of giving back to her country and people," she wrote. "Barbadians have an expectation of this young woman. People want to know when will Rihanna hold a concert for her people in Barbados. They also want to know which local charities she is involved in. It would serve her well to recognise that to whom much is given, much is expected!"

A flood of readers' letters arrived in response. One man claimed, "There have been so many people creating excuses for Rihanna. She knows this country or so I think, and understands our culture and should be speaking out on issues... if she continues dissing our people and the land of her birth in this way, why should we have her as our ambassador? Some way for an ambassador to act!"

However, another reader questioned whether Rihanna's detractors were simply bitter, claiming in reference to the column's headline, "Ask not what your country can do for you, but what you can do for your country? This is a question that Rihanna's critics should be asking themselves. Rihanna's critics appear to be jealous that she is 'hosting parties for her celebrity friends' and not for them."

There were also inconveniently timed media reports of Rihanna's lavish spending, including claims that she was one of just two celebrities ever to have demanded 24-hour security from a police escort for her show in Ireland. The request was denied, with a source claiming, "They told her where to go. The police can't be seen to be giving special treatment to a celebrity when everyone has to queue up in the traffic."

At the same show, held at Dublin on February 26, Rihanna allegedly hired out the entire spa at the Four Seasons hotel for exclusive use – at a cost of €10,000. As well as demanding a flotation chamber, staff claimed that she ran up a bill at the hotel in excess of €100,000 during her stay. According to *The Irish Times*, "Rihanna may have only been around for a couple of years, but she is turning into quite the diva."

Were Rihanna's claims on 'Bad Girl' of being a spendaholic more than just a character – could they have been true to life? Meanwhile, the value of the land the Barbadian government had given her was roughly equal to her expenditure during one short stay in Ireland, a figure which may not have been easy for modest-living Barbadians to swallow. Did they merely envy her €5 million pay cheque, or did they have a point when they asked what she was doing in order that her own country could share the wealth?

According to Barbadian parliamentary senator Irene Sandiford-Garner, however, the land was a small token gesture and – at $100,000 – just a seventh of the cost of placing a 30-second clip advertising Barbados on a US TV network. She also believed that every time Rihanna's face made the front cover of an American magazine, it piqued fans' curiosity about her homeland and encouraged tourism in a more effective and sustained way than an advert ever could.

Describing Rihanna as the country's "most valuable export", Sandiford–Garner argued that, "Someone from among us has come and done what none other has done. No politician, no sportsman, no rum, no doctor, no lawyer is as known throughout the world as Rihanna is. Rihanna alone is an amazing advertising campaign for Barbados, and, as such, we must show admiration and honour her with something meaningful... She is an accomplished young Barbadian woman who deserves everything we can give her as a people."

While these words might have offered Rihanna some comfort, there was even more trouble on the home front when her father humiliated her at her charity concert in Chicago. He had joined her on the road the previous month, after the two had reconciled, and had promised his days of drug and alcohol abuse were over.

But she had let him back into her life only for him to get so drunk that she was forced to book him on a flight back to Barbados. "I acted like a jerk," he told *The Mirror*. "I remember Robyn being really upset and saying, 'Dad, you are going home.' One of her assistants put me on a plane... I know, having regained her trust, I let her down badly by getting drunk."

Estranged from her father and at odds with many of the people of Barbados, it was hardly surprising that the next new material had a darker vibe than usual. 'Take A Bow' – released on April 15 – was a withering putdown of an ex-partner's amateur dramatics, as he tries to convince her that he regrets having a fling. Rihanna dismisses his apologies and assurances that he loves her – to her, it is just a re-run, and she is ready to change the channel. The only thing he regrets, she sneers, is getting caught.

The single went to number one in the UK, USA, Canada and Australia, and was her second single since the release of *Good Girl Gone Bad* to reach the top spot. Less than a month later, Rihanna was in the studio again to record a vocal for Maroon 5. The group had already produced a song, 'If I Never See Your Face Again', but were keen to try something different and add a female vocal. They didn't need to work hard to persuade Rihanna to join them. "I was like, 'Any song – I don't care if it's a song I don't like – I want to do it because Maroon 5 are dope!" she told GMTV.

While she claimed they were her favourite band of the moment, lead singer Adam Levine was focused on her sex appeal as well. "She's obviously beautiful and talented and amazing and I just thought, 'Hey, there's really no better choice! [But] I always find it hard to concentrate [on set] so she doesn't make it any easier!" he joked.

On the video set, Rihanna wore bright red lipstick – a colour that was previously forbidden to her, marking her transition into making music on her own terms. It was a heavily flirtatious video, against a backdrop of a brightly coloured stage which had to be repainted between takes. There was even what one reviewer described as a "sexual chemistry cheerleader" who would call out "Smokin'!" as encouragement between every take.

While *The Guardian* described the scenes as "high-end erotica", Adam told MTV, "It's this kind of ultra-glamorous photography-based late-Seventies, early-Eighties situation. It's really stylish and really beautiful… the most choreographed thing I've ever done."

The video's main selling point was its sensuous sex appeal, and Rihanna played up to the rumours, teasing that Adam was, in a word, "hot" and claiming, "I don't do a lot of videos where I have so much chemistry with the other artist."

According to *The Guardian*, however, their flirting was "professional" rather than passionate – and Rihanna later admitted that the scenes were faked. "It was fun, but it was difficult to get serious for the seductive scenes because Adam and I are friends," she confessed to *IGN Music*. "We would burst out laughing on every other shot."

Unlike Maroon 5's other collaboration, on Kanye West's 'Heard 'Em Say' in 2005, the single failed to live up to expectations, charting at a meagre no. 57 in the US charts. In the UK, it fared slightly better, peaking at no. 28, but it remained the lowest charting UK single of Rihanna's career.

Although Maroon 5 might have lacked urban street cred, Rihanna wouldn't be out of the Top 10 for long. The following month, on June 17, a new version of *Good Girl Gone Bad* hit the shops. It featured the same tracklist as its predecessor, but also included 'Take A Bow' and 'If I Never See Your Face Again' as bonus tracks, in addition to the previously unheard 'Disturbia' and UK bonus track 'Cry'.

In 'Cry', Rihanna plays the role of a hardened anti-romantic, someone who has been hurt in the past and has resolved never to make room in her heart for anyone since. Despite viewing lovers as nothing more than playthings, she suddenly falls in love – with a traumatic ending. Up go the barriers again and she protects herself by promising she will never give her ex the satisfaction of seeing her cry.

As someone who had told the press, "I hate to be vulnerable," and who had suffered tension headaches as a child due to her determination to repress emotion, 'Cry' was perhaps one of the most representative tracks so far of who Rihanna really was inside.

The manufactured mask was slowly coming down, as Rihanna found the confidence to experiment. "I went into the studio making music my way," she told *Digital Spy*. "I found myself all at once."

She continued to take control of her career when it came to 'Disturbia' too. Rihanna was no longer a teenager – she had turned 20 a few months previously – and, although she was still young, she had already sold over nine million albums – more than many artists might shift in a lifetime. She felt she could afford to start experimenting and taking risks now – and she was given added confidence because the track had been given to her by Chris Brown, someone whose musical judgement she completely trusted.

Island Def Jam boss L. A. Reid told MTV: "It was the first time Rihanna actually came to me and said, 'Here's the song I want to put out.' She played me the song. That was her taking control. She understands what hits are and she knows what she wants to say. She's at that place where she can do that."

Chris Brown and his team had originally written the song with his album in mind, but on finishing it he realised it would be better suited to a female vocalist – and his beau was the first person he sent it to. "It's fun being creative and even if you have a concept in your head to write about, you can write it and give it to someone else because it might not personally fit you but it might not be an idea you have," he told *USA Today*.

L. A. Reid didn't need convincing of its commercial potential – it became a single. Once a video shoot was organised, it became the only promo, aside from 'Don't Stop The Music', that Rihanna had a role in directing. The visual theme fitted the lyrics, about a girl who discovers her dark side.

According to a friend of Rihanna's, the video was inspired by the film *Vamp*, starring her idol Grace Jones, in which a victim struggles to escape the clutches of a den of vampires, who hold him captive in a dark underground sewer after one of them has killed his best friend during sex. "Robyn is a huge fan of Grace's work and I believe that film is what gave her the idea for 'Disturbia'. She liked the idea that although the guys had to escape the vampires, they both feared and desired them at the same time. That was the dark side. It seemed twisted."

However, for some viewers, it was a little too twisted. Furious bloggers threatened to boycott the video for its depiction of Rihanna writhing around tied to a chair in a surrealistic gas chamber, branding it unsuitable for children. Others felt that the gas chamber visuals were offensive to Jewish sensitivities. "I wouldn't mind if she was an adult entertainer," one raged. "But she has always marketed herself to children before now, and has a lot of young fans. How am I going to explain this to my seven year old?"

Rihanna's friend gives her side of the argument: "There's nothing creative you can do in life that has meaning that won't offend at least someone. That's what was in Rihanna's head and she's not ashamed."

Despite angering some, the song turned out to be Rihanna's highest chart debut ever in the Billboard Hot 100, moving straight to number 18. It later peaked at number four, making Rihanna one of just seven female artists ever to have two songs in the top five at the same time, hot on the heels of 'Take A Bow'. In the UK, following its release on July 22, it reached number three, despite being made available as a digital download only.

Following the release of 'Disturbia', Rihanna wanted to prove that she was caring as well as controversial by lending her vocals to a charity single, 'Just Stand Up'. The song, which was co-recorded with Beyoncé, Mariah Carey, Fergie, Ciara, Leona Lewis and various other celebrities, donated proceeds to anti-cancer causes.

Rihanna also collaborated with T.I., the American singer most famous for 'My Love', his 2006 collaboration with Justin Timberlake. 'Live

111

Your Life', which was dedicated by T.I. to soldiers battling it out in Iraq, shows him bloodied and bruised, liberating himself from a record deal. It stormed the charts, reaching number two on downloads alone.

However, Rihanna's most notorious single of the year was 'Rehab', her duet with Justin Timberlake. It promised to be an electrifying single from the start, previewed when Rihanna performed it at the American Music Awards on November 23. Wearing an eye patch and black leather elbow-length gloves, she resembled a cross between an S&M fetish model and a pirate.

The official video was equally mesmerising. Dressed from head to toe in leather in spite of the heat, Justin makes his grand entrance on a motorbike, before serenading a waiting Rihanna in the Californian desert. Channelling the theme of addictive love between an inseparable pair, the two look longingly at each other as she drapes herself over the hood of the car.

Pop Sugar praised the video for being "smoking hot", while MTV claimed that it "redefined the phrase 'desert heat'". Of course, Justin's girlfriend, Jessica Biel, was reported to have been unhappy about the seemingly effortless sexuality between them. A source told *Star* magazine, "Everyone was gushing about the intense chemistry between Rihanna and Justin. That's not the kind of news a girl who's waiting on a proposal wants to hear and she was fuming... sick to her stomach."

Chris Brown remained tight-lipped about his feelings on the video shoot, but there was no doubt that his own relationship with Rihanna had reached fever pitch. He had just finished a co-headlining tour of Australia, New Zealand and the Philippines with her when the video was released, and she had been snapped wearing a diamond ring on her wedding finger. Not only that, but the two had visited a tattoo parlour in Australia to get another set inked on their necks, this time matching Grace Jones-style tribal patterns. Allegedly, the whole Oceania tour had been organised for them to perform together because they couldn't bear to spend time apart.

Throughout the year, Rihanna had spoken of dating other men, but it seemed to be a smokescreen to detract attention away from her increasingly intense relationship with Chris. He had been equally nonchalant when questioned about the romance, again insisting, "I'm single. See as many girls as possible!"

Meanwhile, as critics tried to interpret their denials, 'Rehab' stormed the charts, making it to number 19 in the USA and number 16 in the UK.

It was also a particularly big hit in Europe, reaching number three in the Netherlands and number four in Norway and Germany. Plus reality star Kim Kardashian heralded it as the ultimate break-up song.

Everywhere Rihanna went, people were humming the chorus – and she was notorious worldwide for both her singing and her sex appeal. It ought to have been one of the proudest moments of her life. Little did she know that, in the months to come, the storyline would merge with real life and that she would be going through her very own love rehab.

Chapter 6

Soldier of Love

Blood poured from a young woman's mouth as she sat slumped in a car, fighting for consciousness. Bruises, bite marks and tear stains covered her face. This woman had been held in a stranglehold, punched repeatedly, then choked until she briefly passed out. Finally, she had been abandoned by the roadside.

It sounded like the sort of sad story America had heard thousands of times over, with one big difference – the victim was wearing an $11,000 Gucci gown. What was more, the scene of the crime was a $150,000 Lamborghini.

But, America argued, surely such violence was the preserve of drug addicts from disadvantaged families? It couldn't have happened to R&B's most glamorous celebrity couple since Beyoncé and Jay-Z – or could it?

It just had.

Both Rihanna and Chris had been born into similar backgrounds. While Rihanna's father had broken her mother's nose in a fit of rage, Chris's mother was hit so hard by her boyfriend that her nose too had started to bleed. Plus his biological father, a corrections officer at a tough state prison, didn't exactly have a relaxed approach to discipline.

"For the most part, my mom and dad, my biological father, they took

115

good care of me," he told CNN. "But there used to be times when I was scared to go to bed."

Clearly, neither he nor Rihanna were strangers to domestic violence and unhappy home lives. In fact, at times, Chris had been so terrified of the escalating violence that he had also lost control of his bladder.

On *The Tyra Banks Show* in 2007, during an emotional chat with the supermodel, Chris confided that the violence had distressed him so much that he had resolved never to see another woman in pain again. He declared, "Domestic violence affected me, especially towards women. I treat them differently because I don't want them to go through the same thing, or put a woman through the same thing that that person put my mom through." But on February 7, 2009, he broke that promise.

Rihanna had been nominated for that year's Grammy Awards and was eagerly anticipating the prospect of a win. She was also thrilled at the thought of meeting Bono from U2, whose family were big fans, as the two were planning to discuss doing a duet together. A source had claimed, "They will have a chat about setting a formal date to go to the studio together and see what they can come up with. It would be great for Bono to reach out to a younger market through Rihanna and everyone thinks they would be a great team."

It seemed that Rihanna's career opportunities were increasing by the minute and it was with a comfortable smile that she greeted paparazzi at a pre-Grammys party the night before the big event. She and Chris were expecting to be stars of the show although they remained tight-lipped about their relationship. Perhaps they had wanted to protect what they shared from ending up under the media microscope, feeling that their privacy was sacred. On the other hand, perhaps the pair believed it would bode well for their careers to be seen as young, free and single, boosting their appeal with the younger audiences who fantasised about being with them. In reality, they had been in an intense and exclusive relationship. However, it now seemed that Chris was making good his promise to the media of living life as a single man.

Reporters alleged that Rihanna had caught him flirting with the British songstress Leona Lewis, whose hit single 'Bleeding Love' had posed a huge threat to Rihanna's recent chart position, at one point standing between her and the top spot. To say that the two were professional rivals would have been an understatement.

However, according to one eye-witness, it wasn't just being usurped musically that Rihanna had to fear. "He and Leona were laughing and Rihanna saw his hand on the small of her back," a source had told *The Sun*. "It was totally innocent, but that set Rihanna off."

However, as the two made their way back to his rented Lamborghini, it was a text message that really had her temperature rising. The three-page note, reportedly highly explicit, was from a woman asking if she and Chris could meet up later – and it was from someone he had had a previous sexual affair with. Whoever the woman was, Rihanna was furious – and from there, their night descended into chaos.

She later told *Good Morning America*, "I caught him in a lie and he wouldn't tell the truth – and I wouldn't drop it. I couldn't take it that he kept lying to me, and he couldn't take it that I wouldn't drop it. His back was up against the wall. The truth was right there in a text message – and it was ugly."

In fact, the text sparked off a volatile argument –one that would quickly escalate into violence.

According to court documents, an enraged Chris tried to push Rihanna out of the car, but her seatbelt kept her strapped in. Eyewitnesses heard a tearful Rihanna screaming hysterically, then pleading with him as she "tried to get her point across". Chris then began to bang her head against the passenger window and, when she turned to face him, rained punches down on her face. He continued to punch her while he was driving, as blood from her mouth and face poured over her dress and the upholstery of the car. According to Rihanna, she "fended him off with my feet". As soon as she could reach it, she scrambled into her pocket for her mobile phone and left a voicemail for her assistant, warning her, "I am on my way home. Make sure the cops are there when I get there".

This infuriated Chris even more. He responded, "You just did the stupidest thing ever! Now I'm really going to kill you. I'm going to beat the shit out of you when we get home – you wait and see!"

The battle resumed, with Rihanna sustaining bite marks to her ear, arms and fingers. Each time she held her arms up to defend herself, he

117

would bite them whilst punching and choking her, eventually putting her in a headlock. When the assault was over, Chris abandoned the car and fled the scene.

They had appeared to outsiders to be the perfect celebrity couple – musically successful, financially independent, lucky in love and surrounded by adoring fans. But for all their privileges, there was nothing to be envied about this night out. The luxury car that had carried them looked more like a blood-spattered crime scene than a stylish accessory for a star-studded night out.

Abandoned by the side of the road, Rihanna now faced a humiliating walk of shame to safety. "I was battered. I was bleeding," Rihanna told current affairs TV show *20/20*. "I was swollen in the face. So there was no way of me getting home except to get out of the car and walk – start walking in a gown, in a bloody face. So I really don't know what my plan was."

The woman who had once called herself an insatiable shopaholic was now in a very dangerous situation. Her eyes were swollen so severely that she could barely see and she had been close to losing consciousness. What was more, however, she was wearing over $1 million worth of jewellery.

Knowing the game was up, Chris was on his way to the nearest police station to hand himself in, while – fortunately for Rihanna – a passer-by found her and called the police.

An eyewitness waiting to receive treatment at the Cedars-Sinai Medical Centre told the press that he had seen her arrival in the early hours of the morning. "Rihanna was brought through the back entrance on a gurney, flanked by two LAPD officers," he recalled. "It was impossible to know it was her at first because when they wheeled her past me, she had the hood on her fuschia-coloured sweatshirt tightly drawn around her face and she was wearing big brown sunglasses. Rihanna was clearly upset by what had happened and I could hear her screaming."

If she had hoped for privacy, she was to be bitterly disappointed. The nurse might have drawn a curtain across the door of her room and she might have kept her sunglasses on for modesty, but the following day her name was emblazoned across all of the newspapers. There was no way she could escape.

"I felt like I went to sleep as Rihanna and woke up as Britney Spears," she recalled to *Glamour* later. "That was the level of media chaos that happened the next day. It was like, 'What, there are helicopters circling my house? There are 100 people in my cul-de-sac? What do you mean, I can't go back home?'"

Both she and Chris pulled out of their scheduled appearances at the Grammys, leaving organisers to hastily arrange for Justin Timberlake and Al Green to take their places. Rihanna would have to say goodbye to her meeting with Bono and to another year's triumph at the Grammys. In fact, her 'horrific' facial injuries were so extreme that she was forced to pull out of all appearances for the foreseeable future. It was now time for her to withdraw from the public eye until the pain, both physical and emotional, had faded.

As for Chris, the scandal devastated his career. He lost several lucrative sponsorships, including Wrigley's chewing gum. He was then forced to respond to pressure from an online petition by standing down as one of the nominees at the Kids' Choice Awards. Family-friendly radio stations removed his songs from their playlists and refused to be associated with him. Businesses and individuals alike wanted to make it clear that they would not be supporting his actions, making a stand that music industry experts predicted would cost him millions of dollars.

Yet lost earnings in the short term were just a small part of the picture as he faced losing the respect of Rihanna, his first love, and the very fans whose support had sent him to the top of the charts. His previously child-friendly image – which had even seen him perform a song with *Sesame Street* character Elmo – was in tatters; he had gone from hero to zero in just 24 hours. Could his career be over permanently?

Meanwhile, Rihanna was using the time alone to focus on her charity work. Just two days after her assault, newspapers published details of her quest to find a bone marrow donor for a seriously ill five-year-old child. Rihanna spoke out, saying, "She needs a bone-marrow transplant to live. When I saw a video of [victim] Jasmina, it broke my heart. It's so unfair that, for a black patient, it's so much harder to find a bone-marrow match."

The campaign paid off, as Rihanna later elaborated to *Glamour* magazine. "My manager sent me a video this little girl did for her best friend," she recalled of her decision to get involved. "It shows them playing and then Isabelle said to the camera. 'This is my friend Jasmina and here's how you can help her: swab your mouth for DNA and put it into an envelope.' They were both adopted and have the best bond – they are inseparable. The video made you fall in love with both of them. I was like, 'I have to help her.' So I did a bunch of events to raise awareness. Just when we thought we were not going to find a donor, we found one."

The contrast between the two couldn't have been clearer: while Chris was rightly being condemned as a bad example to children, Rihanna was busy saving their lives. What was more, she had the support of the public – as Chris's album sales ground to a near halt, Rihanna's were increasing dramatically.

Even boxer and convicted rapist Mike Tyson condemned the assault, telling MTV, "He's just a baby. He doesn't know how to handle his emotions when it comes to women."

It wasn't looking good for Chris but, as much as she hated to admit it, was there a small part of Rihanna that felt sorry for him? In spite of all that had happened, she faced a long struggle ahead. Before the attack, they had been friends as well as lovers. Should she forgive him and welcome him back or walk away for good?

He had initially shown no remorse, updating his Facebook status with the warning, "You'll begin to see her true colours. Believe it!" However, he soon began to make contact, begging for her forgiveness. Plus, while Rihanna had been flooded with support from furious family, friends and fans, she had also been met with opposition by those who believed she was the one to blame.

Some of Chris's teenage fans had point-blank denied that their much-loved idol could even have been capable of violence. Others posted abusive messages on the internet about Rihanna, insisting that Chris had turned physical because she had provoked him. Unlike the average domestic violence victim, Rihanna was living out her pain so publicly that it wasn't just her ex-lover putting her under pressure – but total strangers too. As well as trying to heal, she had been concurrently fending off an army of devoted Chris Brown fans – and their support for him seemed to be unconditional.

A study of 200 Boston teenagers revealed that just two percent blamed Chris, while a further 46 perent held Rihanna responsible. Another 52 percent blamed both parties. On Facebook, girls expressed their belief that either Rihanna or the tabloids had exaggerated or made it up. "She probably ran into a door," one girl wrote, "and was embarrassed, so blamed it on Chris."

Mimi Valdes Ryan, the former editor of entertainment magazine *Vibe*, suggested that young women's hostility was born out of jealousy towards Rihanna. "His posters are on the bedroom wall, the last face they see before they sleep," she remarked. "They're feeling, 'Why is he with her, not with me?'"

Chris's family also blamed Rihanna for the abuse, claiming that she had lashed out first. His stepfather Welford Hart told *The New York Post,* "When you take off your shoes and beat someone, that's going to hurt. He reacted and tried to get her to stop hitting him, but she kept screaming." For Rihanna's part, she maintained that she had not hit him and had merely kicked out with her feet for self-defence.

Even Rihanna's friends in the music industry seemed reluctant to commit to defending her. While she had enjoyed a good friendship and working relationship with Ne-Yo, he had also headlined a tour with Chris and the two of them were close. He told MTV, "I haven't had a chance to talk to Chris yet. I just want to sit down and talk to that dude. That's still my homeboy at the end of the day. I won't pick no sides."

Meanwhile, although Kanye West had described Rihanna as his "baby sis" and a woman he would "do anything for", he also played down Chris's violence. He implored on VH1, "Can't we give Chris a break? I know I make mistakes in life."

To Tricia Rose, author of *The Hip-Hop Wars*, their apparent lack of loyalty was predictable, if disappointing, and just part and parcel of the 'macho' culture of hip-hop music. "This is the air that hip-hop breathes," she claimed. "The celebration of a stereotype of an aggressive, physical, often misogynistic masculinity that often justifies resolving conflict through violence. It can't be held responsible for this, but it can't be ignored."

Rihanna's father, who had previously made his wife's existence hell with physical abuse, also seemed unwilling to pressurise his daughter to leave her abuser. In fact, he too had witnessed domestic abuse as a child and had perhaps begun to normalise it. "There was never any doubt Rihanna really loved Chris," he told *The Mirror*. "They were best friends and did everything together. People will have their opinions, but whatever road my girl chooses, I will be behind her 100 percent. It's not up to me what she does, but I will support her every step of the way."

He added, "She is a young girl who's always been very stubborn. When she sets her mind on something, she will do it, so it is not my job to try and change her mind. I know she'll listen to her head and heart and make the right decision."

In fact, Rihanna was about to make a decision that, in many people's eyes, was very, very wrong. It seemed that Chris had wooed her back with little more than apologies and a birthday gift of a new iPod Touch. "I was angry, [but] then I got vulnerable and started to miss [him]," she told *News Of The World*.

According to psychologists, this was a classic symptom of an abused woman, where the victim's self-esteem becomes so low that they turn for comfort to the very person who had caused them to need comforting in the first place.

While sources emerged to say that they still loved each other and wanted their relationship to work, newspapers speculated that the pair had taken a trip to Mexico, crossing the border to stay together like career criminals, as depicted in the Jay-Z and Beyoncé duet 'Bonnie And Clyde'. It turned out that Rihanna had holidayed in Mexico alone, but had cut the trip short for a face-to-face chat with Chris in neutral yet private territory – a house that had belonged to R&B star P. Diddy.

Just three weeks after the incident, they had made up and flown to Miami for a weekend away. "It was sort of like a Romeo and Juliet story, like both sides not wanting us to have contact, so we just got away," Chris recalled to *CNN*.

Rihanna cuts a very different figure from the other fashionistas at 2009's Paris Fashion Week in a cropped hair cut, dark sunglasses and a moody all black ensemble JOHNNY NUNEZ/WIREIMAGE

Rihanna fuels rumours of a lesbian affair as she – innocently or otherwise – rests a hand on best friend and assistant Melissa Forde's shoulder at the Rated R album release party on November 24, 2009 at New York's Juliet. JOHNNY NUNEZ/WIREIMAGE

Rihanna looks the part at the Chanel Pret A Porter fashion show at the Grand Palais, Paris, on October 6, 2009 with a beaded black and red Chanel bag.
ERIC RYAN/GETTY IMAGES

Rihanna takes time out in LA to attend a basketball game at the Staples Center, accompanied by attentive love interest Matt Kemp, professional baseball player for the Los Angeles Dodgers. KEVORK DJANSEZIAN/GETTY IMAGES

Is it a giant sex toy or a weapon of mass destruction? Perched on her bright pink cannon, Rihanna shows her enemies she's ready for war in one of her most flamboyant stage shows yet in 2010 in Sacramento, California. MOSENFELDER/CORBIS

Rihanna takes to the stage in the world's most unconventional wedding dress to mark a marriage of two very different music styles, duetting with rapper Eminem at LA's 2010 MTV Video Music Awards on September 12. KEVIN MAZUR/GETTY IMAGES

Rebel Flower: Rihanna lives up to the second part of her nickname by parading a dress adorned with dozens of flowers at the Madrid-hosted MTV Europe Music Awards on November 7, 2010. KEVIN MAZUR/GETTY IMAGES

Rihanna cosies up to Drake for a performance of 'What's My Name?' at the Grammy Awards in LA on February 13, 2011 KEVIN MAZUR/WIREIMAGE

Rihanna dons a policewoman's hat for a performance on NBC's Today show on May 27, 2011 in New York.

Rihanna serenades Staffordshire for a show that reportedly earned her £500,000 at the V Festival on August 20, 2011. MARK SUMNER/REX FEATURES

They spent the weekend jet-skiing and enjoying romantic meals. Yet while Chris saw their reunion as part two of the ultimate love story, Rihanna did not. She might have outwardly shown forgiveness, but underneath she was seething with repressed rage.

"I resented him so much and I always put the tough face on, the 'I can do anything' face, tried to play it off," she told *20/20*. "But he knew. He kept asking me, 'You hate me, don't you? You hate me,' and I would lie and say, 'No.'"

Yet the pressure was quickly getting to her. "Everything about him annoyed me – him being around me, him talking to me. Everything was annoying for me. So finally I just said, 'We can't do this. I cannot continue to do this.'"

Just a few days later, on March 5, Chris was formally charged with assault and making criminal threats and was released on $50,000 bail. Rihanna was distraught to learn that he planned to plead not guilty and, as she read newspaper clippings about herself, began to feel like a fool.

One such report, by *The Sunday Mirror*, cautioned, "Brown has been arrested, but the charges have been built on police evidence rather than a statement from Rihanna, who has refused to cooperate with police. Sadly, this is an all too familiar story. Even if you have pots of money, a brilliant career and a ballsy personality, you can still be reduced to a pathetic, pulverised mess by a violent partner. You just learn how to cover it up."

The report continued. "Think of the wasted opportunity Rihanna had to shop the bastard who beat her up and then warn young women never to let it happen to them. But instead, she's taken her alleged attacker back into her life. Sadly, poor Rihanna has not only lost the battle, but she's lost the respect of all her young fans."

Indeed, when the public learnt that she had given him a second chance, her Facebook page was flooded with comments from angry women, believing she was setting a bad example. "Shame on you, Rihanna!" one read. "He'll only do it again and it'll get worse," another cautioned.

In fact, Rihanna had already had direct experience of that. She had admitted to police officers that this was not the first, but the third attack she had suffered at his hands. It had started off small with an altercation during a tour in Europe, when she slapped him and he responded by shoving her against a wall. There were no injuries to either party on that occasion. The second fight was an argument over a Range Rover, which saw him smash both the front and side windows of the car in a fit of rage.

Yet Chris was still desperate to prove he had reformed, to get Rihanna's approval and to win her heart again. Then his manager, Tina Davis, stepped in to defend his "uncharacteristic" violence. "It was devastating. In all the time I've known him, he's never done anything to make me think that he even had the potential to be violent," she insisted. "He was crying. He told me, 'Tina, I've messed up. I don't know what happened!'"

There was no question in Tina's mind that Chris was repentant. Yet the real question was: did he genuinely regret hurting Rihanna, or was he crying because he knew it was a mistake that would kill his career? Was it her he felt sorry for – or simply himself?

The Mirror was cynical about his motives, suggesting, "Forgiveness from Rihanna would clearly be good for business." It was alleged soon afterwards that his management team had proposed a deal called 'Project Mea Culpa', where Rihanna would be entitled to a $10 million payout if Chris so much as squeezed her arm again. It was a damage limitation exercise, aimed at improving his chances both in court and in saving his career. The deal allegedly included a clause where the two of them would appear on US chat shows together to discuss Chris's recovery and his anger-management counselling sessions. Not only would this give him an opportunity to show the public that he had changed and that Rihanna had forgiven and forgotten – valuable in rebuilding his tarnished public image – but it would also provide publicity for them both.

Finally, if Chris wanted a chance to genuinely repair things with the girl he loved, it could be a good starting point. However, the *Daily Mail* reported, "That might be a tempting offer if it weren't for the sickening suspicion that if Brown was going to lose $10 million, he's unlikely to stop at a wrongly squeezed arm."

Rihanna was equally suspicious. The accusations that she was setting a bad example to the domestic violence victims among her fans hadn't escaped her conscience either. As she was a public figure, she felt it was no longer just her life at risk, but the lives of those who might follow her example by choosing to keep violent men in their lives. Even if Chris did clean up his act and never laid a finger on her again, other people who had been repeatedly abused by unrepentant boyfriends might not be so lucky if they stayed.

It was a battle of wills for Rihanna between the last remaining shreds of loyalty she had to Chris and the guilt she felt at the prospect of speaking out against him – especially if he went to prison – and the need to tell the truth and be a role model for her fans. Without testimony from her or an acknowledgement of guilt from him, he could go unpunished. It was in Rihanna's hands, not his prosecutors, to control his fate – and that was the hardest thing.

The world's eyes were on her, willing her to make the right decision. However, the speculation ended when her attorney, Donald Etra, revealed that she was prepared to give evidence against her ex. "She is planning to do everything the law requires her to do," he told *US Weekly*. "If she is required to testify, she will do so."

Rihanna later explained her decision – both to testify and to close the door on her relationship – by saying that her loyalty lay with her fans. "When I realised that my selfish decision for love could result in some young girl getting killed, I could not be easy with that part. I couldn't be responsible for going back," she told *20/20*. "Even if Chris never hit me again, who is to say that her boyfriend won't? Who's to say that they won't kill these girls? These are young girls and I just didn't realise how much of an impact I had on these girls' lives until that happened."

Chris directly contradicted her, claiming that they could have set a better example by staying together once he had reformed. "We could have made it bigger by saying, 'Look, we're going to both get counselling and we're going to show that domestic violence is wrong,'" he told *The Times*. "Being back with me didn't have to say that, in such situations, the girl should go back to her man, even though he might end up killing her. While I could see where she was coming from, I didn't agree with her. I think it was a drastic statement."

However, Rihanna didn't believe he could change – and she wasn't prepared to wait around to find out. As a special feature about the motives behind domestic violence in *Psychology Today* explained, "An abuser is morbidly insecure. S/he has little sense of his/her own social value and makes an effort to gain or regain some semblance of that value through domination and control. The fear that feeds that insecurity has two fronts: fear of not being lovable and fear of appearing weak. The paradox here is that the abuser is, in fact, weak, which is why s/he abuses – to maintain a sense of control in the first place."

Those traits were exactly what Rihanna had seen in Chris. She told *W* magazine, "When people are insecure, they become very controlling and they can get very aggressive and, in turn, abusive. It doesn't have to be physical. Like, they would say bad stuff to make you feel lesser than them just so that they could have control in the relationship. It takes a big toll on your emotions and on your everyday life."

For all of these reasons, Rihanna felt her best option was to end the relationship. She moved out of Chris's LA mansion and started house-hunting for a new place – one with a $5 million price tag. While she scoured the Hollywood Hills for somewhere she could finally call home, she also made a visit to the Bang Bang tattoo parlour to have a gun motif etched on her skin. It was her official message to the world that Rihanna was no longer a victim – she was a fighter.

However, what came next would take all of the fight Rihanna had left. One morning, she woke up to find a photograph of her bruised and bloodied face emblazoned across celebrity website *TMZ*. Within hours, the image had circulated across all of the major news networks and it seemed as if there was no-one who hadn't seen Rihanna at her worst. There was no chance of denial either – this woman had a visible tattoo of Roman numerals on her neck, clearly identifying her almost beyond doubt. For Rihanna, this was far more than just photographic evidence – it was also an unwanted memento of her pain.

"It was humiliating," she told *Glamour*. "That was not a photo you would show to anybody. I felt completely taken advantage of. I felt like people were making it into a fun topic on the internet and it's my life."

To make matters even worse, the picture had allegedly been leaked by the people Rihanna should have been able to trust the most – the police. "It was a confidential case by law," she told *The Observer*, "so when it became about getting a cheque and completely disrespecting somebody else's privacy, it was just disappointing. I expect that from *TMZ*, but if the police can't protect you, then you can't be safe. You just feel completely exposed. And I was very disappointed, especially when I found out that it was [leaked by] two women."

Rihanna's father, who by that time had been estranged from her for over a year, approved of the picture's release – despite the pain it caused – because it raised awareness. "It's good and bad to see the picture, because there were other people who were thinking [her injuries] might not be that bad, just a little spanking or something," he claimed.

When a celebrity rights group, STOParazzi, heard about the breach, it campaigned for a law to be made in her honour called Rihanna's Law. It would stamp out the release of photographs, particularly by law enforcement agencies, that could exploit crime victims. Under US law at that time, leaking photographs of a sensitive nature came without penalty, provided that no money changed hands for them. STOParazzi argued that, regardless of whether or not they were purchased, distribution of crime photographs should be banned altogether.

While she was grateful for the support, Rihanna was so embarrassed that she withdrew altogether – not just from the prying eyes of the news agencies, whose coverage she usually enjoyed – but from her friends as well. "It's like they are too close to you," she told *20/20* later. "When you have to talk about something so painful, they are going to get too emotional, and that wasn't helping me because I already felt the same way, and I'm looking not to feel like this. I felt like, 'If I'm going to tell you something, and you're going to have pity for me, then I'm not going to talk to you.'"

Some of Rihanna's friends would burst into tears when she tried to talk about it, while she preferred a more stoical approach. "I put my guard up so hard," she told *Rolling Stone*. "I didn't want people to see me cry. I didn't want people to feel bad for me. It was a very vulnerable time in my life and I refused to let that be the image. I wanted them to see me as, 'I'm fine, I'm tough.' I put that up until it felt real."

Meanwhile, she felt that she could be herself with new celebrity friend Katy Perry. The two were total opposites – Katy saw Lolita as a fashion icon and styled herself as a teenage girl, with pastel pink, love hearts and cotton candy featuring heavily in her stage shows. Meanwhile Rihanna wouldn't be seen dead in anything "too girly", and believed herself to be mature beyond her years. In fact, although Rihanna was four years younger than Katy, it was her who played the image of the older, more tough girl – cool, calm and always in control.

Their friendship seemed even more ludicrous in light of the frosty reception she had given Katy's beau, UK comedian Russell Brand, on their first meeting. "He was interviewing me on TV," she recalled to *Cleo* magazine. "I was sick and it was the worst interview I've ever done. I was throwing up in a bucket and a doctor gave me a shot in my butt. Nothing was funny to me. I thought it was the most stupid fucking interview I ever did in my fucking life. [I thought], 'Why am I talking to this idiot?' It made me want to throw up again."

In spite of her awkward start with Russell, Rihanna had instantly bonded with Katy, and she appreciated her relaxed attitude to the turbulence in her personal life. There were no tears or dramas with Katy – just good, old-fashioned fun.

"I don't think I really, like, reached out to her," Katy told MTV in response to reports that the pair were inseparable and that she was offering Rihanna counsel in her time of need. "Of course I consider her a friend, but it's not like, 'I'm there,' making a big deal out of it because I feel weird about that type of stuff. I'm trying to always be there for my friends [anyway]." She added, "We're both on this crazy rollercoaster [of fame] and it's nice to have good girlfriends. I pride myself on having cool chicks in my life and she's a cool chick."

Katy even joined Rihanna on a trip to Barbados to see her family and to take her mind off Chris. Evan Rogers, the producer who'd discovered Rihanna all those years previously, also tried to be subtle about how terrified he was for her well-being, an experience he described as "watching from arm's length". "There were times when I absolutely feared for how much she could handle, when I worried, 'Is she going to melt down?'" he told *W* magazine. "Me and my wife were like her surrogate parents. We've tried to learn how to let go, but there were definitely times when we wished we could go back in time to when things were simpler."

That wouldn't be yet awhile. The fall-out of the fight had been both painful and expensive. Police had seized various items in evidence. Rihanna had been begging for the return of the $1 million diamond rings and earrings she had hired, while Chris's rented Lamborghini had been impounded at a cost of $2,000 per day. Yet the bruises would fade, the money could be repaid – particularly for a wealthy millionaire couple with breathtaking combined earnings – but the emotional pain was another matter. "The physical pain comes and it goes," Rihanna confirmed to *GQ*. "But the thing that stays with you is the emotional scars."

Meanwhile, Chris had armed himself with top celebrity lawyer Mark Geragos, who had successfully defended his idol Michael Jackson on his child molestation trial and had also represented actress Winona Ryder on her shoplifting trial. With a lawyer of his track record and calibre, Chris and his management were feeling confident about the outcome. Rihanna, meanwhile, was simply marking time until the trial would be over.

She had been due to make her first public appearance since the assault on May 5, when she was booked to play the seven-star Emirates Palace hotel in Abu Dhabi. It was cancelled at the last minute due to "inappropriate timing" although, unusually, Rihanna then made a public appearance the following day in London for a duet with Kanye West. Perhaps she simply hadn't wanted to play a concert on Chris's birthday, which also fell on May 5. For the duet, she power-dressed in a man's Dolce & Gabbana tuxedo, with outrageous Grace Jones-style shoulder pads and puff-sleeves, a black bow-tie and a neatly cropped boy's haircut. She was surrounded by supporters, including catwalk model Agyness Deyn, who ran up to congratulate her in person.

However, things wouldn't return to normal for Rihanna until the public furore over Chris had calmed down. To her, every kind face was a potentially pitying one – and the talk about the crisis in the newspapers and on the street was never-ending.

Some speculated on whether it was a win-win situation for Chris, whose name was now on everyone's lips. If he escaped jail, he could slowly regain the support of his younger fans; but if he did time, it could give him added street cred in certain crowds. For example, Akon had boasted about his time in prison during interviews, establishing his identity as an edgy ex-con. His song 'Locked Up', where he donned a bright orange prison uniform and lamented the frustrations of life inside, had been a big hit. However, it was later claimed that he had never been to prison at all and had fabricated the story to make himself appear cool.

With a bit of re-styling, Chris could turn away from his current image – innocent with a hint of naughtiness – and reinvent himself as a tough, edgy artist with experience of the darker side of life. Even if he did time in jail, there was a chance there would still be a place for him in the music industry.

However, hopes of that were dashed at the preliminary hearing before Los Angeles Superior Court Judge Patricia Schnegg on June 22. In the event, Rihanna was not even called on to give evidence. Before any testimony could be taken, Mark Geragos entered a guilty plea to the felony assault charge on Chris's behalf. A deal had been done to keep him out of jail: in return for pleading guilty, his sentence would instead consist both of community service and probation, the extent of which would be announced once the judge had considered the matter in more detail. The end result was far from glamorous.

There was an agonising two-month wait for Chris before he would hear the final outcome, although the judge had immediately placed a restraining order forbidding him from seeing Rihanna, but he resolved to use the time to rebuild his career. British singer Keri Hilson caused a stir when she appeared to trivialise the abuse, claiming that – no matter what he had done – a comeback was just one song away. "It's unfortunate what they are going through, but I feel if you've ever had a fan base, you're really only one song away from appeasing that fan base," she claimed. It was with Keri's help that he would start to record new material for his comeback.

On July 20, he had also broken his silence about the court case. He claimed that legal restrictions had previously prevented him from speaking out but that – against the advice of his attorney even now – he wanted to set the record straight. "I saw first hand what uncontrolled rage can do," he told the world via video link. "I have sought and am continuing to seek help to ensure that what occurred in February can never happen again."

He expressed his deep regret for "unacceptable" behaviour and assured his audience, "I have told Rihanna countless times and I am telling you today that I am truly sorry that I wasn't able to handle the situation differently and better... I felt it was time that you heard it directly from me that I am sorry. I intend to live my life so that I am truly worthy of the term 'role model'."

It was unfortunate timing for Chris – the day that he released the video on his website, he hit the news again. This time, a photographer announced he was suing a member of Chris's security team for assaulting him outside a gym as he tried to take pictures. Chris was also wearing a pendant with the slogan 'Oops' in his online apology – an action some might have thought was insensitive and trite, suggesting he wasn't taking his offence seriously. At around the same time, explicit naked photographs of Rihanna emerged on the internet – something many suspected was Chris's doing.

The following day, July 21, he posted a new song on his website called 'Changed Man', to prove otherwise. It featured lyrics such as, "The world hate Chris" and "Can we love again?" along with phrases that begged for forgiveness, which he hoped would melt Rihanna's heart. His plan worked. Hearing, "I remember your touch, God, I miss you so much," it was something Rihanna found hard to shut out.

In fact, the song seemed to charm her so much that she agreed to meet him. It was rumoured that they violated his restraining order to spend the night together in Manhattan's Trump International hotel. It was an unstoppable, insatiable, logic-defying love – but it was that same blind passion and, according to Rihanna, "obsession" that seemed to have led to the violence.

Her mother Monica spoke to the press for the first time ever to express her terror, and to caution that her daughter was "playing Russian roulette with her life". She added, "I'm devastated. Chris has power over her. She still loves him."

"It's embarrassing," Rihanna told *20/20* later of the relapse. "I was so far in love, so unconditional, that I went back. It's humiliating to say this happened. To accept that – it's a traumatising experience."

She added, "It's pretty natural for that to be the first reaction. You start lying to yourself. The minute the physical wounds go away, you want [the whole] thing to go away, you put it in the back of your head and you start lying to yourself subconsciously."

Just weeks after their clandestine meeting, they were back in the Los Angeles courtroom on August 25 to hear Chris's sentence: five years probation and six months of humiliating community service. The terms of his probation were strict, banning him from drinking alcohol or even visiting bars. The probation was also designed to minimise the risk of them falling in love again, forbidding Chris from coming within 50 yards of her – or 10 yards if they were performing at the same event. A breach of those conditions could result in a prison sentence for the full term of his probation. He was also required to attend domestic violence counselling sessions for a year.

During the sentencing, Rihanna – dressed all in black and wearing pearls – was sheltered from Chris in a private room. When he left the court after a short 15-minute hearing, she was summoned before the judge separately to hear the terms of the restraining order – one that left no chance of rekindling the affair. The outcome left neither in any doubt – for the next five years, contact was totally prohibited.

Meanwhile, on the day of the sentencing, the video for Rihanna's new single 'Run This Town' was released on iTunes. Not only was this a tactical marketing ploy intended to make the best of a bad situation, but the video also served the purpose of showing Rihanna's victory over Chris. While he was receiving his punishment, she was planning her freedom – and reminding anyone who was watching that she was no victim.

The song was for Jay-Z's eleventh album, *The Blueprint 3*, which featured both Rihanna and Kanye West as special guests. The two were chosen for their dominance of the charts, as Jay-Z explained to DJ Tim Westwood: "We basically run this town... myself, Rihanna and Kanye. It's pretty much it."

The video saw the three channelling a powerful, glamorous and in-control gangster vibe. The director was keen to evoke a tribal atmosphere, something very dark and slightly dangerous. "There's a militia, a march and a kind of rambunctious energy to it that, for me, I immediately wanted to tap into," Anthony Mandler told MTV. "I showed some references from the classic rebellious zones of the world. We live in a very orderly society in America, but when you get into Brazil, you get into the Middle East, you get into Africa, you get into Eastern Europe, when you get into places like that, there's a different sort of 'We run this town.' There's less order and more chaos. So we looked at a lot of those references, new photos and historical photos, to capture that kind of falling apart feeling."

After studying the photos, they decided to use torches and bandanas to advertise their swagger. "We wanted you to feel uneasy throughout the piece," Anthony continued. "We wanted there to be a constant layer of tension… and things happen off screen that you don't see. I think people are really going to flip on this."

He wasn't wrong – it made the number two spot in the American charts and sailed to number one in the UK, making it Jay-Z's first ever number one as a lead artist. The tables had turned – when Rihanna first started out, he had been the star, but now she was the one helping him to score hits.

The song also demonstrated the unity the two had against their enemies: while lyrically it could have been a veiled threat to Chris – many believed already that his career in the music business was over. Jay-Z had previously informed MTV icily, "Chris is a dead man walking. He messed with the wrong crew." Rihanna was on the winning team – not only was she running the town, but also the charts.

In a final twist of the knife for Chris, the week Rihanna hit number one in the UK singles chart – her highest debut yet – he began his community service. While she was celebrating the song's success, he was about to embark on the biggest reality check of his career. Dressed in a bright orange high-visibility vest, he crouched down to clear police-horse stables in his home town of Richmond, Virginia. Rihanna was enjoying the sweet smell of success, while he had to be content with eau de horse manure.

What was more, his position afforded him little privacy. Onlookers stopped to snigger at his neon orange uniform – and to watch one of

R&B's top-charting performers reduced to clearing litter. A handful of fans also arrived and were rewarded for their loyalty with a sheepish grin and an awkward wave.

For Rihanna, it should have been finally over; but in reality, for both parties, it was just beginning. Now that the court case was closed, the restrictions were lifted on discussing it – and there was an expectation that both would speak out. Just a few moments of ill-advised anger had precipitated months of pain, the emotional scars lingering and long outliving the physical ones. However, one good thing that had come from all of the speculation was the opportunity for the public to learn from it.

Journalist Leslie Morgan Steiner, who wrote the book *Crazy Love* about her experiences living with a violent partner, believed Rihanna's case had turned some of the myths about domestic abuse on their head. Steiner was herself the antithesis of a stereotypical victim, being a financially independent, Harvard-educated career woman with high self-esteem, a loving family and a good network of friends, and she saw that Rihanna could not be typecast either. In her eyes, it proved to the world that abuse could happen to anyone – rich and famous or poor and downtrodden. "I thought it only happened to poor women with children and without options [before it happened to me]," Steiner explained.

Newsweek concurred: "No amount of money or fame can protect you from the terrible cycle of emotional dependence, shame and fear that keeps people with abusive partners. Women who are abused look for ways they may have 'provoked' an attack, finding fault with their own behaviour to explain the unexplainable – why would someone they love hurt them?"

Steiner also believed Rihanna's case overturned the myth that a man who had been a victim of abuse in the home himself would not repeat the same mistakes. Recalling her own experience, she said, "It never occurred to me, all the times [my partner] shared his very painful stories about how he was abused as a kid, that he would hurt me. I never felt fear. I only felt sympathy. I didn't understand that cycles of violence are passed from generation to generation."

Rihanna told *20/20* of Chris's outburst, "He forgot the pain he experienced with his mom." However, perhaps it wasn't that simple – and Leslie hoped it would raise awareness that victims of violence might need professional help to keep them from acting out their pasts, so that they could vent any repressed anger about their childhoods safely.

When Rihanna told the world she had lied to herself about the severity of the abuse, it represented what many experts saw as a typical facet of an abused woman – denial. If she denied there was a problem now, though, she would have the rest of the world's protestations to contend with too.

"Since denial is the most dangerous thing about domestic abuse, the fact that this happened in a public way will make it very hard for her to go back into that relationship," Steiner commented. Restraining orders aside, she believed that Rihanna's nightmare was probably over for good.

All of the song lyrics that had started as fiction had now become alarmingly true to life. 'Take A Bow', where she lamented that a lover wasn't sorry, but was only sorry he'd been caught. 'Cry', where she said she didn't want anyone to see her sorrow, that she had her barriers up against love. Even the unreleased 'Electric Guitar' – the duet that wasn't to be – had references to bleeding and killing in the lyrics that the two could never have imagined would become real when they wrote it. Together, Chris and Rihanna had told their own fortune.

Both appeared on TV separately after the sentencing to talk over what had happened. On *20/20*, Rihanna spoke of how she saw her best friend and first love turn from a gentle boyfriend to an enraged aggressor, recalling, "He had no soul in his eyes. He was clearly blacked out. There was no person when I looked at him."

She also revealed that her first instinct when the news broke was to protect him. According to her, his emotional state was so fragile that she also feared he would commit suicide. "The world hates him now – his fans, his career, he lost me – I just need to let him know, 'Don't do anything stupid,'" she added.

In spite of her sympathy, she seemed less moved by the video apology he posted on his website, noting that it sounded as if he "might have been reading off a teleprompter". "I just didn't know if he understood the extent of what he did," she claimed. "The thing that men don't realise, when they hit a woman – the face, the broken arm, the black eye, it's going to heal. That's not the problem. It's the scar inside. You flash back, you remember it all the time. It comes back to you whether you like it or not, and it's painful."

She also talked of her anguish when not only fans but Chris's cousin Phylicia Thompson came out in public to defend him, saying, "Chris was not brought up to beat on a woman, so it had to be something to provoke him for Chris to do it."

Rihanna responded, "It's ignorance... that makes it OK for him to do that to me? They kind of give an excuse for what he did."

Meanwhile, on September 2, Chris appeared on CNN to give his version of events. It had been a stormy few weeks for him, with media reports emerging to suggest he had broken his probation just four days after sentencing when he was seen in LA nightclub Guys and Dolls, celebrating avoiding jail time, ironically. Many had disapproved, using this as evidence that he was not remorseful.

However, on CNN he painted a very different picture. "I never fell out of love with her," he stated. "When I look at it now, it's just like, 'Wow.' I can't believe that happened. I was distraught. I went to my mom and broke down. Of course I remember what happened but it was and is still a blur... I guess that night is just one of those nights I wish I could just take back and I really regret and feel totally ashamed of what I did."

He added, "That's not who I am as a person and that's not who I promise I want to be. I'm pretty sure [Rihanna and I] can always be friends, and I don't know about our relationship, but I just know definitely that we ended as friends."

Despite his unreserved apologies, he also caused controversy when he lashed out verbally at chat-show host Oprah Winfrey for urging Rihanna to take some time to heal before considering going back into the relationship. She had warned on her show, "Love doesn't hurt – and if a man hits you once, he will hit you again." Outraged, Chris exclaimed, "It was a slap in my face. I did a lot of stuff for her, like going to Africa and performing for her school. She could have been more helpful, like, 'I'm going to help both of those people.'"

Aside from his outbursts, which some insiders felt were the nail in the coffin of his rapidly deteriorating public image, he was also missing his lover. He wrote on his Twitter account, "My heart is incomplete."

While Rihanna responded to his public pining by telling the world that she too still loved and cared about him, there was no turning back for her. The *20/20* TV interview was something she had been reluctant to do, but it helped her to move forward. "At first I completely shut down," she confessed to *W* magazine. "But now I feel like this happened to me so that I could be a voice for young girls who are going through what I went through and don't know how to talk about it."

In the month following the assault, Rihanna had been surrounded by friends, but no-one that had personally experienced her plight and, even in her large crowd, she felt totally alone. She had turned to God for healing and even believed that fate had put her in that position so that she could act as an example. The interview had consolidated all of her feelings and had allowed her to turn her pain toward others' benefit.

"It was the biggest weight lifted off my chest," she told MTV. "That was my first real time opening up. I had a lot of tension bottled up, so when I finally spoke about it, it felt really good. More importantly, it felt good that people got something positive out of it… it's not fun to talk about or listen to, but there are a lot of women who are going through it, a lot of teenagers who are scared to talk about it. So I thought it was a good thing that I can be that voice for them and help them get out of that situation."

Meanwhile, she delivered a stark message to anyone who might be dealing with the same thing: "Stop blaming yourself for that outcome. There's nothing you can do, ever, to excuse a man's behaviour like that."

Chapter 7

Battlefield Chic

In just one night, Rihanna had gone from a chart-topping artist who was known for holding the number one spot in the charts for 10 weeks running and for having, in 'Umbrella', the world's most popular tune of the 21st century, to one who was better known as a pitiable victim of domestic violence. Her court case had spiralled out of control until her name was more synonymous with battery than record-breaking hits. It was miles away from the strong and self-sufficient Rihanna she wanted to portray – in fact, she didn't want to show her weaknesses and imperfections to her nearest and dearest, let alone the whole world.

"Rather than people forgetting about it, all everyone kept going on about was that night," she told *The Mirror*. "It really got to me – that was all people wanted to talk about. There wasn't a single day when I wasn't followed by people wanting a piece of me. Then there was all the talk and gossip on the internet and it wasn't anything I could control or avoid. I just tried to live my life, but it was hard. I was in the spotlight for all the wrong reasons. Whereas once it was about my music, now all the attention was focused on what happened to me. But then, with any big life experience, it makes you more resilient."

Both parties had learnt a lesson. Chris had been reduced to pleading with fans to buy his albums, publicly begging, "I need your help."

139

Meanwhile, Rihanna had learnt that fame meant much more than the designer dresses, diamond earrings, glamorous parties, sell-out arena tours and widespread adoration she had fantasised about since childhood. It carried much more responsibility than that – and, at the tender age of 20, she had already found that out.

Following the assault, Rihanna found refuge in the studio. After being kept busy on the road with a constant stream of concerts, interviews, rehearsals, choreography sessions, signings and photo shoots, she was accustomed to full days and couldn't bear to be idle. "I started to go crazy after about a month in the house, so I went back to work," she told *W* magazine. "The mic was my therapist. With the mic, there were no negative comments, no negative energy."

She resolved to pour out all of her thoughts and emotions into her new album – to be called *Rated R* to demonstrate that she wouldn't be censoring herself. The album would become her boyfriend, best friend and counsellor all wrapped into one. While she told *News Of The World* that all she wanted for Christmas was "great sex and great food", she was willing to let that go so that music could be her great love affair, conceding, "I would put love on the side for what I do because it means so much to me."

Like Lady Gaga, who once claimed, "It's really your job to have mind-blowing, irresponsible condomless sex with whatever idea it is you're writing about," Rihanna was making love to her music too. Her main focus for her energy – sexual or otherwise – was the new album and that was just as well, because it was time-consuming and exhausting. "*Rated R* is like a child," she informed *Access Hollywood*. "It needs a lot of attention and it's a lot of hard work and sleepless nights."

Not only had she put her all into it, but it promised to be her most personal album yet. "I wasn't just singing lines," she told *The Mirror*. "Every word meant something because it was my story. I was venting my personal issues."

Yet, apart from teasing snippets from songwriters, no-one knew what the album would sound like. Collaborator Ne-Yo warned, "Expect an edgier and almost angrier Rihanna," while Jay-Z kept a tight-lipped silence. Rihanna enjoyed hearing the speculation – the focus was off her assault for once. She hoped her comeback would change things permanently, rewriting the script of how she was perceived. It had taken just a day to crush her reputation, so she hoped it could be remedied equally quickly. "I don't want that five years from now, every time they see Rihanna, they think of Chris Brown beating me," she told ABC. "That's not who I am."

However, Rihanna wasn't the only one planning a triumphant return. Chris was back and his inconveniently timed nationwide tour of America would start on November 14, just two days before Rihanna's own comeback at London's Brixton Academy. While her new album was about love rehab and emerging a fighter, Chris's was about career rehab – and both hoped to move on.

Yet while Rihanna wanted to forget the drama, letting her new material speak for itself as the last word on a trauma she longed to forget, Chris was ready to talk – in agonising detail. While he might have been repentant, he now had a demeanour of defiance too. "This is a bad mistake I made, but... I don't believe I should let it shatter my life," he told *The Times*. "I feel I have no reason to go through the rest of my life with my head hanging down."

He also took the opportunity to condemn women for their role in domestic violence, insisting that there were two sides to every story. "Domestic violence is totally wrong whatever the circumstances, no exceptions," he stated. "But a lot of people think it's a one-sided issue, i.e. only men on women. Let's give an example: I'm not saying verbatim it's what happened, but if a woman hits her man, it's looked on as if it's him not being macho. It's kind of laughed at, like, 'Ha ha, your girl beat you up! Not much of a man, are you?' But if a man, let's say, were to defend himself or to use force, then he's wrong... it's always a mutual situation though. I feel if force is being used by both of them, then both are wrong."

Although he didn't state that he was referring to his own relationship with Rihanna, she had confessed to police officers that she had slapped him several months before the incident that had ripped them apart. She had also told a radio station that, in a fit of temper, she had once hit her brother hard enough to leave a bruise during an argument, using both a bottle and a phone. However, she had been clear that she had not struck Chris on the night that he punched her.

Chris's comments seemed to confirm the view that hip-hop music was surrounded by a macho culture, which normalised the use of violence in order to appear tough. He also seemed to argue that abusive relationships ran in families. During his counselling sessions, he said, he had been told that 30-40 percent of reported domestic violence involved female aggression. He argued, "That figure could be even higher, because what guy is going to find it easy to come out and say, 'Yeah, my girl beats me'?"

However, on hearing this, some of Rihanna's fans might have repeated the statement she gave when asked what she wanted Chris to do next. She had told *20/20*, "What I want is for him to accept the responsibilities and not find a way to feel sorry for himself."

Meanwhile, he inferred that the incident that had seen pictures of Rihanna's bruised and swollen face circulated around the world had been good for him. Talking of the rehabilitation process for his public image, he told *The Times*, "It's humiliating, yes, but that in itself is good... being brought back down to earth is no bad thing. It makes you appreciate anew how lucky you've been."

He went on to say that the experience of his first album going to number one had propelled him into an unrealistically "arrogant realm" that he had to come back from.

He was no longer love-struck. Months earlier, he had been posting messages about his adoration of Rihanna and his sincere regret, but he now felt he had moved on. He claimed that Rihanna's TV interview, where she claimed that he had left her emotionally scarred, terrified and ashamed to ever have dated him, had made him focus on himself instead of love. "That interview put things into perspective for me," he told *The Times*. "It just really made me focus on me. I was too focused on love. There's nothing wrong with that, but sometimes love can make you lose sight of your goal, of what your purpose is... I'm not heartbroken right now. I'm moving forward. I will always be remorseful for the situation, but at this point I'm just living my life."

His interviews had been candid, but it wasn't so much what he said that was revealing as what he didn't say. On his third album, *Graffiti*, released in December 2009, songs like 'Changed Man' had been omitted from the play list altogether, replaced by others such as 'Famous Girl', which lyrically throbbed with anger and accusation towards a mystery woman in the public eye. Even more uncomfortably, 'Wait' featured an ill-advised sexual pun on the word 'beating' – not the ideal lyric for a man who had just been convicted of assault.

However, he was now moving on via domestic abuse counselling, which he stated was making him a better person. "It's a domestic violence class, but there's also an anger management element that helps you to deal with situations and gives you certain do's and don'ts... It's a blend of group therapy and learning how to manage your feelings. It's character building."

Meanwhile, his live shows, billed as a "fan appreciation tour", would see him donating part of the proceeds to the Jenesse Center, a domestic violence shelter based in LA. The public questioned whether he was motivated by album sales, a search for love and approval, or the urge to become a better person; but, as for Rihanna, it was clear that her aim was to bring the spotlight firmly back to herself and her work as she contemplated performing her first solo live show since the attack.

To prepare, she released a promo video for the song 'Wait Your Turn', from her forthcoming album, but retitled "The Wait Is Ova". In it, she sang about pitching with a grenade, as if to signal that she would be taking no prisoners from the very beginning. But her new material had a harder edge, with 'woman scorned' written all over it and, looking to spice it up with a rockier sound, she invited guitarist Nuno Bettencourt from the rock band Extreme to join her on tour.

It was a risky move: rock could be an elitist genre, with some musicians reluctant to be associated with a mere pop artist whose music they couldn't mosh to. So when Rihanna's musical director Tony Bruno invited Nuno to be her lead guitarist, he was passing on the message as a matter of courtesy – no-one was holding their breath for an instant "Yes."

"My first thought is that [she's] probably not the greatest fit for what I do," Nuno blogged. "But Tony said, 'Before you say no, let me play you the direction she wants to go live.' And when I heard it, I said, 'Wow, this rocks!' It's heavy and funky – and it hit me that this is *my* shit, this is my style, how I love to play. I got very excited at the possibility of playing some of her great songs with a heavier treatment. When I asked Tony why, he told me that Rihanna loves bands like Paramore and Linkin Park and loves to push it up a notch in the rock department."

Although Nuno was better known for his work with punk rock artists like Perry Farrell of Jane's Addiction, the proposal was difficult to turn down. "Let me think, touring and sharing the stage with a cool and talented artist like Rihanna and being able to bring what I do passionately to the table as a musician and performer? I'm *in*!" He added that it would be a "great opportunity to blend our talents to create a high-energy experience".

While he confessed he might have lost some rock'n'roll street cred by collaborating with someone who had never heard a rock song when she first hit the charts, and whom everyone in the rock industry was calling a 'pop tart', he was defiant about his decision, telling *Globe*, "There was always a difference between her and the Britneys of this world."

She proved that when she released the album's lead single, 'Russian Roulette', on November 7. She still had sex appeal, but this time it was more dangerous. While the single cover featured Rihanna clad in nothing but barbed wire, the video was equally grisly. It showed her writhing helplessly in a torture chamber, getting run over by a car, drowning underwater, getting slowly gassed and even masturbating as she tries to evade her captors. The sound of a heartbeat was vamped up to sound threatening and mysterious, while Rihanna's shivers and whimpers reminded listeners of the fragility of life, proven at the end by the final gunshot.

But what was Rihanna's sinister comeback all about? The song pointed to violence in relationships, it showed Rihanna both aroused and terrified simultaneously, and the song title used the same words as her mother's public warning when she reunited with her ex – that she was playing Russian roulette with her life. It was inevitable that people would make the Chris Brown connection sooner or later.

However, according to song writer Chuck Harmony, the public had been too quick to judge. "Whatever she came out with, if she came out with 'I still love you,' that would have been about Chris Brown. If she came out with 'I hate your dog,' that would have been about Chris Brown too. It's just a natural reaction for people to associate," he claimed.

Meanwhile, co-writer Ne-Yo was equally cagey. "I didn't really want to go there too much, because I know that's what everybody's expecting," he told MTV. "I don't think there's a person alive that doesn't know what happened or what it was. I don't feel it needs to be glorified… it's sad that it took that happening to get it the attention it deserves. Women get beat up all the time and no-one says anything about it. But now that it happened to a celebrity, it's 'Let's talk about it on Oprah Winfrey.'"

He added, "Chris Brown is a friend of mine and I don't view him as a bad guy for what happened. It was an absolute mistake and he has some lessons to learn and some maturing to do, but I'm not going to bash him for that. I'm not going to turn my back on a person I call a friend because he made a mistake. I can't write the Chris Brown bash song and then turn around and look myself in the mirror."

However, the two writers had wanted to make a track that reflected Rihanna's growth, and they couldn't ignore that her life had been hell that year. With that in mind, they felt a bubblegum pop track wouldn't be appropriate. Instead, they sought a sound that was "a little darker, a little edgier, a little more morbid".

It was that sound that gave her a Top 10 hit around the world, reaching number two in the UK, number nine in the USA and number seven in Australia. Plus, although she had been better known for her assault than her songs in recent times, her comeback gig at London's Brixton Academy on November 16 would soon set the record straight. "There was nothing of the victim about her as she dragged attention back towards her music with all the spectacle she could muster," *The Evening Standard* reported. *The Mirror* agreed: "Rihanna was reborn fiercer than ever last night."

Ten days later, the album was released and Rihanna's transformation was out for the world to see. She had taken her image up a notch: whereas the photographer of her last album, Roberto D'Este, had said the brief was for a sexy look rather than a vulgar one, Rihanna had been more daring with *Rated R*.

On the album sleeve, she adopted an 'S&M chic' look, appearing in barbed wire again. "I wanted to do things that weren't done before," she told *Universal Music Malaysia*. "I came out with the idea. I just come out with crazy things when I'm sleeping."

She also did the one thing she promised her mother she would never do and posed naked, her modesty shielded by a 'Censored' sign, while photographers snapped away in the background.

The artwork was shot by Ellen von Unwerth, a feminist photographer known for bringing out women's erotic potential, and Simon Henwood, a creative director who helped her discover and project her subversive side. "My references are always dark," he explained. "I always look at someone's work and try to find the twisted truth. I think because of what she had been through recently, she was open to playing with this. I got to do some pretty dark stuff, which for an artist of her status is rare."

Indeed, the mainstream music world might have been saccharine sweet and wholesome, with most of the top artists happy to conform, but Rihanna wasn't playing along. The album sleeve also featured Rihanna wearing a dress made by countercultural fashion designer Hussein Chalayan, who was also known for sending models down the catwalk wearing headscarves while they were totally naked from the waist down. His rebellious interpretation of the demure Muslim headscarf had caused endless controversy. However, his taste for controversy was perfect for Rihanna, whose heavy black eyeliner, sultry poses and liberal nudity came in total contrast to what fans were expecting.

Aside from Grace Jones, one of Rihanna's major style icons this time around was Lady Gaga. According to *The Observer*, "Gaga doesn't do pretty, or available, or submissive, or obviously glamorous. Instead she does scary, she does theatrical, she does brave... there is something Bowie, something early Madonna-esque about the way Lady Gaga wields her sexuality. Something unapologetic, unflinching and shameless in the very best sense."

Like Gaga, Rihanna cared more about portraying a tough, untouchable image than one that would attract men. Both defied the conventional stereotypes of what female showbiz stars should look like – Gaga with her outrageous outfits that could border on the grotesque at times, while Rihanna refused to doll up with the crowd-pleasing formula of long hair and girly dresses. Both stood out from the crowd and both shared an inspiration – Gaga adored Grace Jones too.

Rihanna told the *News Of The World* of her respect for Gaga, gushing, "We're not normal, we're artists. We're the craziest people who live. We're very sucked up in art and we don't give a fuck who likes it or who hates it, because it's what we live and breathe. I respect more than anything people who are not afraid to be themselves."

However, her 'uncle' Evan, who was involved in producing the album, admitted to being "uncomfortable" with her newfound freedom – both for sales reasons and to protect the girl he was as close to as a member of his own family. "This album was sort of like hearing your daughter use profanity for the first time," he told *W* magazine. "I'm not going to lie and say I didn't worry about how her core audience would react."

Yet all that mattered to Rihanna was that she was expressing herself for once. She co-wrote nine of the 13 tracks on the album and let her emotions run riot – the good, the bad and the ugly.

"It was really personal," she told *W* magazine. "It was from me in the most authentic way. It's like a movie, in that when I was making this album, every day I was in a different mood. Sometimes I was pissed off, sometimes I was miserable and every song brings out a different story."

However, while there were a variety of tales to tell, none of them were love stories. Rihanna began to reject other people's ideas – something that would have been unthinkable when she started out – and turned down eight ballads to shake off the role of a love-struck victim. "It was exactly what I tried to stay away from," she insisted. "When I was about to start the record, that was the first thing I said: I don't want no sad songs, I don't want no songs about love. I don't want to do that – that's totally expected."

L. A. Reid, the boss of Island Def Jam, was delighted – although not surprised – to see Rihanna coming into her own. "She's not looking to be a consensus builder," he claimed. "She's not looking to see what the room thinks – the people who work with Rihanna execute what she thinks."

Yet it had only been three years since Rihanna had publicly stated she shied away from the studio decisions, claiming, "I don't like to be too much in control or too dominant".

Ne-Yo had also noticed the change, recalling to MTV, "When I first worked with her, she was very – I don't want to say obedient, because it sounds like you're describing a dog – but she would take my suggestions without question. She trusted me, which was cool, but I told her I ultimately wanted to get to a point where she would give me input, where she'd be a collaborator and not a puppet – and now I think we've gotten there. She's showing parts of herself that she didn't show before because she didn't want to scare anyone off. She's experienced some pain now and it's helped her grow to a point where she's able to explore it."

She was beginning to make other demands too. Not only was she not prepared to make an album full of love songs, but she also wanted to turn away from commercial pop and instead turn up the bass for a rockier sound. For L. A. Reid, it was a welcome change to work with someone who knew what she wanted to achieve – and he believed it was the next stage in her evolution. "What I expected was for her to make a statement with the album," he explained. "It's all about having artistic expression and having a point of view, rather than being a little pop girl that you give songs to."

Her transformation might have bewildered long-term fans who were used to a more demure Rihanna, but she was undeterred. "It's shocking for them," she told *Universal Music Malaysia*. "Even the sound from my album was a culture shock for them. But fans appreciate honesty… they can always tell when something isn't sincere. At first they might be intimidated by the image, but after that they really get into it. They love the music now, they love the image. After a while they just notice that this is just really who I am. It's not really going to stop people from saying negative things about who I am. I can't really change who I am."

For the first time in her career, her album seemed to be a strong reflection of who she was inside. She was no longer a cookie-cutter pop star, but a woman who had been through a trauma: it wasn't colourful rainbows and romantic sunsets she was portraying, but intense and sometimes dark emotions. She still had a team of talented producers at her disposal, but this time she was heavily involved when it came to writing the lyrics.

'Madhouse', the first track on the album, warned away those who were easily scared, while, as already mentioned, 'Wait Your Turn' was a slice of grenade-touting swagger with a Jamaican twang. However, things really got started with 'Hard'. The same duo who had brought her 'Umbrella' flew all the way to Paris to present Rihanna with the song and she was instantly enthused. "It had such an arrogance to it, which is so far from who I am, which is part of why I wanted to do it," she told MTV. "It was fun. It was bragging – a lot of attitude."

On 'Hard', she delivers scornful threats to any woman who might have been eyeing her throne, reminding them that, with fan mail from 27 million, the top is far more than a holiday destination for her – she is there to stay. Rihanna also recruited the rapper Young Jeezy for some added bravado and swagger.

The 'Umbrella' team also gave Rihanna 'Rockstar 101', which was a tribute to the decadence of the rock'n'roll lifestyle. Not only did it tread similar ground to Beyoncé's 'Hip-Hop Star' musically, but it had a matching theme, bringing out an unexpectedly daring side to both singers.

Her writers ventured a little out of their zones too. Although Ne-Yo had claimed he would never help to write a song that criticised Chris Brown, he might have got pretty close on 'Stupid In Love'. He and Stargate penned it as a break-up track in which, despite being desperately in love, Rihanna couldn't excuse her man's behaviour.

'Firebomb' is another unapologetically bloodthirsty revenge song, talking of petrol-bombing someone and shooting bullets into the tank of their car. Tellingly, Rihanna fantasises about smashing the front windows of a vehicle to avenge a lover – exactly what Chris did to her during a fight. "I recorded a song about revenge," she confirmed to *News Of The World*, "wanting to put someone through what they've put you through, so they can finally understand why you can't forgive them."

The violent imagery might have seemed extreme to anyone who wasn't passionately involved in a toxic love affair at the time they heard it, but it fitted the context of Rihanna's experiences perfectly.

Another perfect fit was 'Cold Case Love'. In the past, many song themes had been nothing more than role play for Rihanna – here, however, she was singing every word from the heart. One of the most emotional tracks of the album, it almost rains pain. She talks of a love that broke the law and needs to be investigated and, feeling love shouldn't hurt, she wants to be released from her prison. Rihanna had described her relationship with Chris as "dangerously obsessive" and addictive love affairs, according to popular psychology, are known as open prisons. Victims can leave but, no matter how bad things get, their tormentor maintains a hold over them. Here, however, Rihanna is finally finding the courage to break away – and 'Cold Case Love' is the soundtrack to her liberation. The song has the distinctive Justin Timberlake sound, seeming to emulate his 2006 tune 'Until The End Of Time' – and sure enough, he is credited with co-writing the tune.

In 'G4L', the preoccupation with vengeful violence that saw Rihanna get guns tattooed on her torso weeks after the Chris Brown attack strikes again. Another building block for her tough-girl persona, she promises to be a gangster for life – and a perverted one at that, if licking the murder weapon to prove that revenge tastes sweet is anything to go by.

Non-aggressive love songs were a tough taboo for a fiery Rihanna to contemplate during the recordings. "I didn't want to let my guard down and let people in," she told *News Of The World* of her open wounds. "I didn't even want to talk about love."

However, will.i.am from The Black Eyed Peas persuaded her otherwise when they duetted on 'Photographs'. The song captures a nostalgia-tinged few moments of regret, where Rihanna flicks through all that she has left of an ex she never wanted to part with – an album full of pictures. A partner piece to will.i.am's collaboration with Cheryl Cole on '3 Words', it is one of the few songs on the album that conforms to a traditional pop sound.

She was also persuaded to tackle love with a twisted edge on 'Te Amo', the tale of an lesbian love affair that leaves her intrigued but reluctant. The song's title comes from the Spanish words for "I love you," which Rihanna's character initially struggles to understand,

150

and symbolises both the mystery of the relationship and the lack of understanding outsiders have of the dark attraction between the pair.

On 'Rude Boy', Rihanna unveils her penchant for bad boys – but only if they can keep up with her. The tune gives a nod to dancehall and Jamaican culture, with Stargate adding a commercial touch.

Finally, Rihanna exorcised the final remaining demons from her relationship with Chris on 'The Last Song' – one that was so painful, she was reluctant to record it. It symbolised the very last goodbye – not just formally, but in her heart as well – to a love affair. It was the moment she had been waiting for, yet it was so nerve-wracking that she would keep pushing back the recording – until it was last on the schedule. "When the label finally said we had 12 hours to turn in the album, I was like, 'OK I have to do it,'" Rihanna recalled. "I just drank some red wine, dimmed the lights, got in the booth and sang it."

As the recordings drew to a close, she had squeezed out every last drop of emotion; now the media would have something new to talk about, rather than reminding her of the assault constantly. "It's relieving... I finally got to let go and move on," she told *GQ* magazine. "I wanted people to move on with me, because the last big thing they know about me is that night – and I don't want that to be what people define me as."

After the recordings, Rihanna also started to find peace in her heart. She had gone through so many bullets with her ex-lover's name on them that finally there were none left. "[At first I felt like] 'What did I do to deserve this? Why was it backfiring on me?'" she told *The Mirror*. "[But one day] I was in New York and I woke up and I just knew I was over it. It was a different day. I felt different. I didn't feel lonely. I felt I wanted to get up and be in the world. That was a great, great feeling."

Rihanna had refused the help of a therapist on the grounds of pride – apart from one occasion prior to her TV interview about the assault, when her management had put her under pressure to let her emotions out. While it had released her anxiety, she wasn't about to make a habit out of it. In her hometown, therapy was regarded as either an unnecessary luxury or a humiliating cultural *faux pas* – so the album had been a good way of venting metaphorically without having to bear all.

Plus, she had been able to control what she said and how she expressed it. Pictures of her ordeal had been broadcast around the world, but her emotions had been the one thing she was able to keep private.

All in all, using music as therapy had been a good experience for her – and what was more, she believed she had grown as a person. Shortly afterwards, she added to her tattoo collection with the phrase, "Never a failure – always a lesson."

"If I was afraid to make mistakes, I wouldn't be where I am now," she told *Bravo Germany*. "You learn through making mistakes. I got my tattoo written backwards on my collarbone just because of that. I wanted to remind myself every day when I look in the mirror."

The phrase could just as easily have applied to Rihanna's father too, who claimed his crack cocaine addiction had made him realise how much he loved his family and couldn't bear to lose them, giving him the strength to kick the habit. The logo probably mirrored many situations in Rihanna's life, but the one she had in mind at the time had been her ill-fated affair with Chris.

"As traumatic and as terrifying as that was, and sometimes I wish it never happened, my whole life changed in the most amazing way after I went through that," she told *The New York Times* of the assault. "If I didn't go through that, I swear you would've been interviewing a completely different person."

There were still times when it all became too much – such as an album launch party for fellow artist Jay Sean which took place on the same week her own CD was released. Rihanna was guest of honour at the event and £100,000-worth of Cristal champagne was flowing to celebrate. A mammoth amount of free booze might have been a good way to impress a woman who seemed to have it all, but it became less of a party and more of a bash when a Chris Brown track was played by the DJ. She wasn't going to grin and bear it – instead, she got up and left.

Another incident occurred at the Pepsi Super Bowl concert on February 4, 2010, where she shared the billing with artists such as Timbaland and Justin Bieber. Justin was the typical hormonal teenager – he had his eye on Cheryl Cole, Kim Kardashian and Vanessa Hudgens all at the same time – but he had an especially soft spot for Rihanna.

According to rumours, he had been telling organisers at various events that he would only appear if a meeting with Rihanna was part of the package. His amorous attentions might have been irritating for her, but she saw it all as a harmless teenage fantasy – after all, she was just a few years older than him. However, besides fending off admirers – all in a day's work for a glamorous singer – she also received a potentially terrifying flashback of her violent attack at the after-show party.

She had been relaxing at a table with Timbaland and Kim Kardashian when several bottles of champagne came hurtling past, narrowly avoiding hitting her before smashing into pieces at her feet. According to the press, the bottles were "potentially deadly" and every time one landed, the drunken revellers responsible had been yelling "Touchdown!" to get into the Super Bowl spirit. The DJ stopped playing Rihanna's track and evacuated the party, screaming, "Everyone get the fuck out – Super Bowl is ruined!" To make matters worse, Chris nearly broke his restraining order inadvertently when the pair came within a few feet of each other at the same club.

Another awkward moment came when she was reported to have landed a part in a film called *The Last Dragon*. She would have the opportunity to act out her ruthless and vengeful fantasies as a dominatrix in the martial-arts flick, starring alongside Samuel L. Jackson. There was even a planned trip to an S&M sex dungeon so that Rihanna could get into character and learn more about the subculture.

However, she was left startled when hip-hop artist Bun B from the group UGK suggested that Chris Brown played the leading role. "He's got the baby face, he's got the build," he was reported as saying. "And if none of this would have happened, he still would have been Rihanna's boyfriend. Let me tell you, he's not a little dude. Chris is six-foot two. He's very athletic and once they would have put him through the ringers and taught him some of those moves… and he's quick as shit too. I'm telling you, he would have killed this movie."

However, Rihanna was still riding on the wave of her video for 'Hard' and was having too much fun to care. Since its release on November 10, 2009, it had shot its way to number eight on the US chart. This was due in no small part to the video, which saw her as a sergeant addressing her army, rolling around in the mud and marching in the desert, as well as straddling her own bright pink tank.

"It's couture military," Rihanna enthused to MTV. "Everything is surrounded by the idea of something military. We have tanks, we have troops, we've got helicopters, we've got explosions... Tight gear, lots of cute outfits, lots of bullets. Crazy."

Like the 'Umbrella' video, Rihanna had been willing to try anything, no matter how provocative – and, according to her director Melina Matsoukas, best known for her work with Katy Perry, that was what made her a delight to work with. "She will try anything, which is always great because you have a lot of artists who won't do what you need them to do," Melina claimed. "She'll go there and I definitely wanted to bring that part of her out – that fun side."

The fun side also extended to her fashion – which was why she sported giant, formidable looking spikes on her shoulders and tribal war paint on her face. "She loves crazy outfits," Melina continued. "She loves the fashion... and [she's] one of the only artists that will take it there and wear it and wear it well. That part is always fun. Nothing looks bad on her, so that's even more fun. She goes with it and she really challenges you to take it a step further with the status quo."

However, not everyone loved the look – and to some, it was downright offensive. According to *About.com*, the video was "one of the most tasteless, offensive moves by a major pop star ever". The reviewer added, "I fail to understand the point of Rihanna humping the gun turret of a pink tank dressed in Mickey Mouse ears... [and] treating the tank as a sex toy."

He saw it as distasteful for glamorising war, but Jay-Z, on the other hand, had been so proud of the song that Rihanna's first performance of it had been at one of his concerts in LA the previous year.

Her next single was 'Rude Boy', also with a video directed by Melina Matsoukas. Released on February 19, the video combined pop-art-inspired animations with both a Grace Jones-style performance and a nod to Jamaican culture. Loud, colourful, provocative and indiscreet, the video had some horrified onlookers grinding their axes and gnashing their teeth. According to the *Daily Mail*, watching Rihanna "in teeny shorts, provocatively pushing her bottom towards a man's crotch as she sang 'Rude Boy'... would sexualise young women in an unhealthy way." Other journalists expressed their discontent at having to explain to their curious preteen children what "getting it up" meant and why it might matter if a love interest failed to make the grade size-wise.

But to Rihanna, who writhed in a skin-tight zebra print body suit in one scene, it was just like many of her other videos – "dark and edgy and tough" and "pretty freaking cool". She went on defiantly to add fuel to the fire by performing the song as part of a medley, along with 'Hard' and 'Don't Stop The Music', at the Nickelodeon Kids' Choice Awards on March 27.

However, in her director Melina's eyes, raising the hackles of a nation was the ultimate compliment – a middle finger up to censorship, even. "When you do something provocative, there's usually a repercussion," she explained. "It's going to be talked about or banned or slandered in some way. But it's making an effect and people are having a dialogue about it, so to me that's successful."

The video for 'Rude Boy' was criticised for less ego-boosting reasons when the team was accused of plagiarism of M.I.A's video for 'Boyz', but the single still made number one in Australia and the USA. It nearly reached the top in the UK too, although Brits were marginally more loyal to home-grown talent, keeping the British-born Tinie Tempah's 'Pass Out' at the top spot.

By now, Rihanna had learnt to toy with her critics rather than let their comments hurt her. In the same month, March, to parody reports that she was "robotic" and "asexual" on stage, she performed at the Echo Awards in Berlin by appearing with two robots.

And her Last Girl on Earth tour would see her taking further control of her image and reacting in defiance to critics' attempts to censor her. "I like to think of myself as the last girl on earth because sometimes people make decisions based on the outlook of others and you know, to me, my life is my life. It's my world and I'm going to live it the way I want to," she told *Entertainment Tonight*.

She proved that as her tour hit the UK, when, according to *The Financial Times*, fans learned enough about her state of mind to "keep an army of psychoanalysts busy for months". Besides that, she had promised a "daring" high-budget set of performances like nothing her fans had seen before. There would be no clean-cut Beyoncé-style stage shows.

"We've never done a tour to this capacity," Rihanna confirmed to AOL. "The production is unbelievable and the costumes... we just took it to a whole new level. Visually and sonically, it's going to be a big step up from the last time. We just keep growing."

The build-up to the UK tour wasn't without incident – on April 19, her show in Zurich saw her taken to hospital with a rib injury. Narrowly avoiding a breakage, she recovered just in time to play the next night's show in Lyon, France.

However, on the opening night in the UK, at Birmingham's NEC, it was business as usual for Rihanna when, according to *The Daily Telegraph*, she had "shed most of her clothes by her second song". There was more in store than PVC and latex though – she was on the war path. There was more performance here than the average TV action drama, with knife-wielding dancers, visuals of bombs exploding, half-naked men in First World War helmets and bright pink tanks all forming part of the action. It might have been an authentic visual of war – if army officers carried dominatrix drill sergeants as a matter of routine. But then, not many war-mongers carried a six-piece guitar band with them either.

Some loved and it some loathed it – for Rihanna's part, she was simply mixing war with glamour and making violence decadent, just as many nouveau-riche gangster types had done before, but with her own stamp on it. The garish shade of pink adorning everything from the rifles to the warring tanks implied that Rihanna was still a girly girl at heart and still had her womanly wiles. However, it would be a foolish person who dismissed her as a bundle of maternal softness.

To some, of course, for all her tough-girl posturing, there was a heart of gold inside and she was simply using a violent persona as a defence mechanism against being seen as a victim.

If that was her goal, she seemed to have succeeded. According to *The Daily Telegraph*, she had "sought to escape sympathy or victimisation by comprehensively remodelling herself as a strong woman". Meanwhile, *About.com* insisted, "She projects a dominant female image, which was exactly what was needed to move past the unfortunate Chris Brown chapter in her career."

Her tour wasn't just a visual extravaganza however – like the man she spoke of in 'Rude Boy', it was about more than just looking good. It would be necessary to perform and Rihanna was up for the challenge. Having taken drum lessons from Travis Barker of Blink 182, she played a rendition of 'The Glamorous Life', originally written by Prince for his then drummer, Sheila E, as well as launching into a vocal cover of Oasis's 'Wonderwall'.

While Rihanna entertained the UK, she hadn't left out her Stateside fans, and a promo video for 'Rockstar 101' was released there on June 1. She wanted to portray the rock'n'roll fantasy authentically and had been desperate to get a real-life rock star playing in the video. Ex-Guns N' Roses guitarist Slash performed on the track itself, but Rihanna's first choice for the video was Mötley Crüe's bassist, Nikki Sixx. Sixx refused, writing on his Twitter account that he had "respectfully said no".

Rihanna then turned to Nuno Bettencourt, who told *Globe,* "She had never played guitar before… but she was telling me when I first met her how it was going to be cool doing that live and she was kind of emulating air guitar and I said, 'Why don't you play on it?' She kind of laughed and I said, 'I'll get you to play on the song.' Now she looks better than I do playing the damn thing!"

However, that still wasn't enough for Rihanna, whose thoughts then turned back to Slash. Unfortunately, his schedule was too packed to allow him to do the honours in person. By this point, Rihanna had been rejected by several rock guitarists – some felt she would damage their rock credibility, while others were simply too busy – so she decided to play the part of Slash herself.

"She was really sweet," Slash told *Star Pulse,* claiming that he was flattered by her impersonation. "She sent me this pleading text to come do the video, but I couldn't make it work. I told her that me not being in the video wasn't going to make it or break it."

He added, "The video is way better with her being me than with me being me… all things considered, it brings an element of sexuality to it that I probably wouldn't have been capable of. I think it's hot and I sent her a text telling her it was definitely hotter with her doing it… everything works out the way it's supposed to."

Rihanna was anything but conservative in the video, both donning a wig of long black curly hair and a top hat to emulate Slash in one scene and appearing totally naked in another, her figure smeared with black body paint. Her look outraged parents again, though. "I miss the *Good Girl Gone Bad* Rihanna who keeps her clothes on and still makes good music," one blogged. "Nowadays every singer is trying to be controversial to set themselves apart from the others… sometimes, it's just better to be normal." Another blogger sniped, "If she was so talented, she wouldn't need to try and shock others."

However, Rihanna believed that she was the same person she had always been. She told *Universal Music Malaysia*, "People think my style is too sexy. They always say that. It's not like it's a new thing. I've always been sexy with my clothes, even from my first video. I had on a short top, baggy jeans and with my underwear showing. I was always a little more risky and I like taking risks. I like being bold and brave and daring and that's why my fashion choices are like they are."

Plus, according to *Billboard*, her sex appeal was about to hot up even more – the website claimed that she "saved a far sexier clip than 'Rockstar 101' for her fans abroad".

That track was 'Te Amo', which saw Rihanna being pursued relentlessly by an ardent female admirer. *Digital Spy* referred to the unwavering string of sexy videos by commenting, "Rihanna's taking a well-deserved break from titillating the blokes here – only to find herself the object of another lady's affections." That lady was catwalk model Laetitia Casta and the location was Chateau de Vigny, a French castle that would become a lesbian love den for the pair in the video.

Some groaned that Rihanna was courting bisexuality for all the wrong reasons. Female singers had been publicly experimenting with girl-on-girl passion since at least 1995, when a lesbian artist called Jill Sobule released a song called 'I Kissed A Girl'. It was banned from commercial radio for indecency, but a track by the same title reappeared to a more liberated 21st-century Britain in 2007 via Katy Perry – and they welcomed it with open arms. The track sold in its millions, as did the 2001 song 'All The Things She Said' by Tatu.

However, it turned out that not only was Katy a preacher's daughter who insisted she wouldn't take it any further than a flirt and an 'innocent' kiss in reality, but the Tatu girls weren't lesbians either – one of them shattered that illusion soon afterwards by having a baby. In 2010, Lady Gaga and Beyoncé collaborated on 'Telephone', which saw the portrayal of a fictional – and potentially sadomasochistic – romance between them. Gaga escapes from prison, fleeing in a getaway car with her new lover, who informs her, "You've been a very bad girl." Shortly afterwards, Gaga appeared on the cover of Q magazine wearing a strap-on dildo.

Notably, however, Beyoncé had told the press years before that she could never so much as consider kissing a girl, as she felt it was 'wrong' and against her religious beliefs as a devout Christian. Meanwhile, any chance of a real-life romance between Rihanna and Laetitia seemed to be ruled out by the fact that the latter was married with three children.

So, when it came to Rihanna, was she genuinely bisexual or simply buying into lesbian chic? Did she mean it or was she playing a role and, like so many others before her, just pretending?

New York DJ Angie Martinez had broached the question before the single had even been released when she saw pictures on the internet of Rihanna caressing a female friend's breasts. It wasn't the only one, either. "There are tons of [those pictures] online!" Rihanna laughed. "I don't have a lot, so any time I see a good rack, I grab 'em. Women are beautiful. I'm not into them, but they're beautiful. Girls just want to have fun."

However, despite her denials of being bisexual, Rihanna seemed to have warmed to the idea following the recording of 'Te Amo'. She told *News Of The World* that she had a crush on Cheryl Cole, claiming, "I've met her! She's so hot! I remember in Girls Aloud I'd always look at her because she's the cutest one!"

Her enthusiasm went from light-hearted and lukewarm to fever pitch when she told *The Mirror* about her desire to play the lesbian lover of Megan Fox in a movie. "All humans are born with the ability to be attracted to both sexes," she claimed. "I mean, I could see myself in a relationship with a girl." She added, "I'd love to play [the film role of] an assassin – either that, or a lesbian. Maybe both! Hey, a gay assassin, there's nothing hotter than that. Megan Fox would play my girlfriend, hands down! She's yummy. She's hot."

Was Rihanna stepping up her bisexuality for the 'Te Amo' press campaign or had she always harboured latent desires that had simply grown over the years? After all, she had been a co-writer on the song, on an album she felt was more representative of her than any other throughout her career. The model Tajah Burton later published a memoir of a lesbian affair with an un-named "Barbadian pop R&B artist" who many identified as Rihanna, something Rihanna herself refused to either confirm or deny.

Whatever the truth was, Rihanna had the world talking about her. As for Chris, his career was continuing to self-destruct: he was banned from entering the UK for a tour due to his criminal record for assault and, weeks later, he broke down in tears while performing a cover of Michael Jackson's 'Man In The Mirror'.

Rihanna seemed to have emerged triumphant, especially when mutual friend Ne-Yo donated the profits from his song 'Heroes' to the domestic violence charity, Respect. She also had a new boyfriend, LA Dodgers star Matt Kemp, although whether she had made a good choice was less certain. Felisha Terrell, an actress who had previously gone out with him, chose this moment to claim that he was a violent stalker and that she had taken out a restraining order against him the previous year. In her application for the order, she told of how he was allegedly kicked out of a club for fighting with a woman and how she feared "his behaviour will turn towards me".

In spite of that, it seemed that Rihanna was safe and happy. She made a joke to her make-up artist in one interview, who was asked to use some concealer on a bruise on her leg, "I had some really wild sex last night! Just kidding!" No longer sensitive about the subject of bruises, it seemed she had finally put the past behind her.

Chapter 8

The Scent of a Rebel

Rihanna hadn't just moved on from the domestic violence chapter in her life – she had subverted it too. Fans watched open-mouthed as she and Eminem got together for a very public re-enactment of a dangerous relationship. The song's title said it all: 'Love The Way You Lie'. The track was released on July 4. Within hours, it had millions of hits on YouTube, a figure that rose to 18 million views after five days. It ultimately went on to become the UK's biggest selling song of 2010. But what was it about this track that had everyone's eyes on the unlikely pair?

Rihanna was singing about the fine line between unbridled passion and full-on abusive violence, telling of how a man's anger can sometimes feel like a flattering display of jealous possessiveness. It wasn't the first time pop music had covered such a dangerous subject: as far back as 1962, legendary songwriting team Gerry Goffin and Carole King had written a track called 'He Hit Me (It Felt Like A Kiss)' for girl group The Crystals. In it, the protagonist longs for violence from her lover as proof that she is desirable. When she is seen with another man, she wants him to be angry. She takes his wrath and jealousy as a signature of how much he loves her and without it, she fears he might not love her at all.

The difference now was that Rihanna herself had been a victim of domestic violence – and she had worked hard to make sure that

161

the public's knowledge of what happened to her that night didn't overshadow her work as an artist. Why, then, did she want to record this song? Perhaps she needed to explain the ins and outs of violent relationships herself. Popular theory saw them as volatile, attention-seeking dramas between two co-dependent partners who in reality are both deeply insecure. The psychoanalysts might have tried their best to unveil the mysteries of abusive relationships, but who better to explain than two people who had both been through it themselves?

Eminem, too, had hit the headlines years before by writing a murder fantasy and naming it after his wife, Kim. The song starts as he coos at their baby daughter sleeping on the sofa but quickly turns dark when he discovers his wife has cheated, destroying his fantasy of a perfect family. That's when the violence begins.

Treading the fine line between twisted love and extreme obsession, he repeatedly tells her he hates her, before breaking down when he realises how much he loves her. That doesn't stop his fury though, as he drives her to a remote spot and tries to push her out of the car. Strangling, screaming, slapping, hair-pulling and knife-brandishing follows. Finally, choking sounds are heard, while Eminem screams: 'Bleed, bitch, bleed!'

It might have seemed shocking, but it was reality – in some relationships, these extremes of anger really happen. And the sheer volume of record sales suggested that some people, somewhere, were relating to it.

The truth of the complex, troubled emotions at the core of the song was rooted in Eminem's relationship with his sometime wife, Kim Scott – the couple have to date been married and divorced twice. No matter how many times he publicly humiliated her, telling the world of how he beat her and would do it again, she couldn't bring herself to leave. For her part, Kim never participated in the mud-slinging, but – rather like Rihanna in 'Rude Boy' – she did go on the radio to criticise his sexual performance. The two would break up and then reunite, always returning to each other in the end. What was more, it wasn't Eminem's fame that compelled Kim to stay – they had been sweethearts since their early teens. Theirs was a true-to-life dangerously addictive relationship.

Rihanna was intrigued by what was in Eminem's head, telling MTV,

"He's just so mysterious. It makes you curious as to what's going on in his world. I feel like I could ask him a million questions in a day."

She also felt that collaborating with him on a tune about abuse was her chance to express herself. "I knew if he sent me a record, there must be something to it," Rihanna told *Access Hollywood*. "It couldn't just be, 'Oh, duh! She was in that relationship, so we have to get her!' The lyrics were so deep, so beautiful and intense. It's something that I understood, something I connected with."

Yet what would the public make of this and what could they learn from it? Were the pair excusing violence, condoning it as part and parcel of a passionate love affair, during times when one provokes the other? Or were they holding a mirror up to the ills of society? Either way, they had the music world hooked.

In the video, Eminem is ready to wreak the ultimate act of revenge, whatever it takes – if he can't have her, no-one can. While their house bursts into flames, set on fire by Rihanna's jealous lover, he raps a plea for her to take him back. While he promises to change his ways and never lay a finger on her again, both seem to acknowledge that he is lying. It portrays that his behaviour is somehow sexually or emotionally addictive enough that she would risk her life to stay by his side.

Some domestic violence groups were frustrated, feeling that the video was undoing all the efforts they had made to promote the message that love shouldn't hurt. After all, the video featured two of the world's biggest music stars, as well as Megan Fox, an actress renowned for her sex appeal. It was bound to be a mainstream production, so would it normalise violence for the masses? Some critics compared it to the Jessica Alba-fronted film *The Killer Inside Me*, where she is beaten to within an inch of her life by a man who exchanges sweet nothings with her in the process. Her last words before she loses consciousness are, "I love you." Jessica then told the press that her character was a woman with a "death wish" who had "finally found a man who was man enough to go through with it".

To some, it portrayed bloodthirsty beatings as an acceptably macho expression of love. *The Daily Telegraph* commented that "one might have received more progressive views on the topic from [murderer] Raoul Moat". Critics felt that big-budget movies were glamorising violence without a thought for those in everyday abusive marriages. Those who might have been downtrodden and who stayed in their relationships due to poverty, shared children or fear of reprisals – did they love the way it hurt?

Others disagreed, believing that Rihanna and Eminem were providing a voice for abused people by portraying what was real life for them. For some, it was even romantic, portraying a love that had self-destructed but was nevertheless a strong and genuine love – one where the pair would do anything to be together. Perhaps it brought a type of humanity to both parties, illustrating that desperate and painful emotions were harboured by both – and that they simply needed help.

Meanwhile, Rihanna refused to be criticised for talking about something she had once been a victim of herself. She told *Access Hollywood*, "It's something that we've both experienced on different ends of the table. [Eminem] pretty much just broke down the cycle of domestic violence and it's something that people don't have a lot of insight on."

They had now. The song debuted at number one on *Billboard*'s Digital Songs chart, while it made it to number two on the UK singles chart. It reached the number one spot in Denmark, Norway, Sweden, Canada, Ireland, Australia and New Zealand too. She had even made chart history as far away as the notoriously conservative South Korea, where the tune was the third best-selling song ever by a foreign artist.

But to make sure that fans got a balanced view of events, Rihanna then recorded a second version, 'I Love The Way You Lie (Part II)', which would appear on her fifth album and which featured herself in the lead vocal, therefore demonstrating the viewpoint of both sides.

Why did girls like Rihanna love the way a man lied? According to scientific research, passionate love and snorting a line of cocaine both activate the same part of the brain. That section is also said to be responsible for controlling addictive behaviour patterns, explaining why love might become an addiction in itself. Meanwhile evolutionary psychologists countered that by claiming that staying in an abusive relationship harked back to caveman times, when abandonment in the wild would mean almost certain death.

The theory stated that a little light violence in a man, whilst hardly desirable, might have been an evolutionary advantage to a partner, serving as an advertisement of her mate's ability to fend off rivals and protect her, therefore deterring unwanted attention. Apparently, protection was once vital at all costs, even if it meant a daily barrage of bully-boy tactics. There were numerous theories to explain the problem. Rihanna, however, was no scientist – she was simply explaining how it was for her.

She didn't have much time to pay attention to the backlash, however, as she was locked in the studio, frantically putting the finishing touches on her fifth album. She had enjoyed an almost continuous presence in the charts for years, because – unlike some artists who took long breaks in between albums – Rihanna barely stopped.

These recording sessions were especially hectic because she had been simultaneously recording her scenes for her first big-budget acting role, in the science fiction film *Battleship* – based on the game of the same name and starring Liam Neeson – which is due for a 2012 release.

Probably fearing a lawsuit, the film's director, Peter Berg, had taken the precaution of offering a weapons expert on the first day of filming to save Rihanna from inadvertently blowing her own head off. When she heard, she roared with laughter. "I was weapons trained in the cadets as a teenager," she exclaimed to *The Times*. "I march, I shoot, I do drill. My role in the film is to be the bad-ass who knows how to handle the arms [but] that's not really acting for me. I am a bad ass in real life."

She demonstrated that from the very start of filming, assuring *Billboard*, "They always want me to sit down when the dangerous stuff happens, but I am a control freak – so I said, 'No.'" She added, "My favourite part has been shooting in the ocean. We were going at top speed and I had to shoot this really bad-ass weapon off the front of the boat. There was gunpowder all in my mouth by the time it finished." Madonna might have worn shoes with a revolver-shaped heel, but Rihanna was taking military chic to the next level, shooting weapons herself instead of simulating them. She had also been bragging about the pistol tattoo on her torso, telling the world that it symbolised "power and strength".

As if to prove her own strength, in between filming and recording her new album she was also still touring the world with her giant pink tank. And she wanted to bring everything together and capture the fighting vibe on CD. While terrified assistants followed Rihanna every step of the way on the set of *Battleship*, willing her to stay safe, they needn't have worried. There were far more harrowing conditions ahead. Earning multi-million-dollar pay cheques hadn't made recording sessions any more glamorous, or less time-consuming. A cramped bus in the middle of urine-soaked car parks was her makeshift studio while on tour when, exhausted from her latest concert each time, she would spend the early hours of the morning recording too.

"We took a studio bus on tour and after every show, we'd sit in an empty car park until 5 a.m. and record," she told *The Sunday Times*. "Then we'd get back on the tour bus and sleep for a few hours. Every afternoon I had acting classes; every evening, a two hour show, then another studio session. Some of the car parks reeked of piss. One I'll remember until the day I die. It smelt like truckers had been peeing there forever and I had to run between buses holding my breath!"

She might have been tough on herself, but Rihanna was every inch as tough with her writers. She was demanding hits that were tailored to her – ones that were like no-one else's sound – and to make sure she got them, her team employed over 100 producers and songwriters and sent them to work in writer camps that were almost as nerve-wracking as summer camp for cadets. Even veteran producers such as the Stargate duo described their working conditions as "extreme".

"We gave them guidelines and a bunch of topics," Rihanna told *Billboard*. "We'd have 10 writers in one room and five writers in another room and put them with one producer, then split the group up and put them with another producer."

Rihanna was setting the bar higher on this album. She would have some old friends taking part in the sessions, who'd written for her numerous times before, but there would be no favouritism. There was no guarantee that their songs would be picked unless they had a sound that set her apart from the rest – one that could "only be Rihanna".

"I didn't want the generic pop record that Ke$ha or Lady Gaga or Katy Perry could just do and it'll work. I wanted songs that only I could do, that had that little West Indian vibe to it, had that certain tone, a certain sass and certain energy," Rihanna told MTV. "It's easy to croon to a tune that just about anybody else could sing."

A loose-lipped Rihanna was forced to explain herself when the quotes hit the internet. Was she dismissing her peers as talentless manufactured pop acts without a sound of their own? She tackled the accusations head-on in an interview with the German magazine *Bravo*, insisting "Katy is my friend! I would never diss her. I don't see her as my rival. My only rival is myself, because I always want to get better and better. I meant all the producers that give singers like Katy, Lady Gaga and Ke$ha always the same kind of pop songs. They think, for sure one of them will take it and make it a single. They don't realise that every one of us has their own style."

She believed that, for some producers, success was defined by a tried-and-tested pop sound. For example, Katy Perry's 'California Girls' and Ke$ha's 'Tik Tok' both dominated the charts at the same time, shared the same co-writer and had a similar sounding hook. "It's easy to get a dance beat and just throw a song on top of it and call it a hit," she sneered to MTV. Both tracks sold in their millions, but Rihanna was looking for something more.

"The most important thing is to be happy and true to yourself," she told *Marie Claire*. "I don't want to look back at this 30 years from now and say, 'I did it all to make them happy and I didn't enjoy it.' I want to be able to say people loved me because of who I am… the album is the most true Rihanna album in terms of the sound and the energy and the look and the vibe of it and the lyrics and the West Indian twang. Everything about it is tailored to me and nobody else could have done any of those songs, which is why I love it!"

One of those unique songs was the Caribbean flavoured 'Man Down'. Recently, Lily Allen and Gwen Stefani had been the only best-selling artists in the public eye to experiment with reggae, although they had moderated it, blending it with pop for a more watered-down sound. Rihanna wanted an uncompromising pure reggae sound – not a diet version – to hit mainstream playlists and 'Man Down' was her pick.

Contrite one minute and swearing blind that if she's taken for a fool she will reach straight for her firearm the next, Rihanna plays a colourful character, dealing with her emotions at shooting a man dead. However, like 'Unfaithful', the murder was a metaphor for the lesser crime of destroying a man's life. "It's about letting a guy go and breaking his heart," she told *The Times*. "I would never use violence. Anyone who has been through heartbreak knows the pain is as real as a gunshot."

Had Rihanna ever been desperately in love, only to have her heart broken, or was she as yet too young? She had once described Chris as her "first real love", but she later told *Glamour* it "would be really annoying" if she failed to find "the one" in the next 10 years and reached the age of 31 without ever having fallen in love.

She took a more light-hearted look at love on 'What's My Name?', a "young and playful" ode to a man who can't put a foot wrong in the bedroom. Feeling that the song wouldn't be complete without a special guest to play the mystery man, Rihanna took control of finding a collaborator – and the one she had in mind was Canadian actor and hip-hop artist Drake. Her approach was just as forceful as it had been with the 'Umbrella' writers – and her persistence paid off. She cornered him backstage at an event and demanded that he listened to the proposed song there and then. Co-writer Tor Erik Hermansen, one half of Stargate, told *Billboard*, "She's calling me up saying, 'Where are the files?' That's one thing you don't often hear from artists on her level."

Rihanna elaborated. "Drake is the hottest rapper out right now… he's the only person I thought could really understand the melody of the song and the minute he heard it, he said, 'I know exactly what I'm going to do. I love it.'" The rest is history.

Meanwhile, some musical blending saw a mixture of country-style rock and reggae with a good-time vibe on 'Cheers (Drink To That)'. If an Alabama country and western bar had been swept up in a music-related earthquake, in the style of Michael Jackson's 'Black Or White' video, and hurtled towards Jamaica, this is what it might have sounded like. Samples of Avril Lavigne's 'I'm With You' added the light rock sound of a stroppy Canadian's teen pop to the mix.

'Raining Men' also has a Caribbean twang, aided by ballsy rapper Nicki Minaj. What was more, should Rihanna grow tired of the endless shower of available men and wish to put her umbrella up, Nicki might be interested. "We're not getting cozy yet," the US rapper joked to an interviewer. "There is a possibility because she's just a bad bitch. That'd be like a freaking crazy power couple right now in the world of females."

Rihanna pushes the boundaries a little further with 'S&M', when she audaciously reveals a penchant for whips and chains. However, it's not all police sirens, salacious sex practices and hook-ups – there are also some tender moments on the album.

'Fading', aided by a sample of Enya's 'One By One', is a smooth soul number recalling the moment when Chris finally became a part of her past, while 'Skin' is a breathy bedroom-style ballad featuring a long guitar solo at the end.

'California King Bed' is a rock-tinged anthem more reminiscent of family-friendly stadium rock than Rihanna – but her intention was to keep listeners guessing. 'Complicated' is a song with hints of Kelly Rowland's sound, addressing a boyfriend who makes himself incredibly hard to love.

Finally there was 'Only Girl In The World', which would be Rihanna's first single from the album and represented her new, fearless persona. Released on September 10 2010, it peaked at number one in 16 countries, including the USA, UK, Australia and Canada. Meanwhile, her style had changed just as much as her sound. "Lots of people dress like Gaga now," Rihanna told *Billboard* breezily. "I've just stepped off into a whole new look and style."

Part of what had turned her away from her previous look was seeing everyone wearing the same outfits. "The whole shoulder pad thing and the architectural look is so sharp-edged and tough," she claimed dismissively. "I'm over that. I like floral prints now, which I never liked [before]. Trends are boring – it's boring to see everyone doing the same thing."

There wasn't much chance of Rihanna conforming or blending in, but as a precautionary measure – and to stand out from the crowd even further – she had also adopted a bright red hair-do, styled in long wavy locks. "It feels really loud and liberating," she added. "It's not a very quiet colour and it grabs a lot of attention, I have to say, whether it is positive or negative. But I love it… it is really expressive and daring. It is also fun to have your hair be a ridiculous colour. It is so out of the ordinary."

Not for much longer – to her surprise, fans flocked to hairdressers all over the world to ask for the Rihanna look. Fans' fascination with recreating her style might have frustrated a woman who couldn't abide trends, but she was flattered when company after company started to come forward and ask her to be the face of a brand-new Rihanna-fronted fashion line. She had abandoned her famously boyish image for a more feminine one, anxious for her look and sound to "scream being a girl" – and stores were keen to get in on the action.

However Rihanna didn't want to be part of anything in name alone – she felt that having a keen eye and over 500 pairs of shoes – and an alleged status of second biggest spender ever in Barney's NYC store – qualified her to be the boss. "I should have a range already, but I'm stubborn," she explained to *The Sunday Times*. "Lots of companies want to stick my name on a range and hand me a big cheque, but if it's my name on it, it should be me designing it."

She showcased her new look on the video for 'Only Girl In The World', which found her alone in a desert flaunting floral-print clothes and giant faux pink roses. "We shot landscapes that we found a couple of hours outside LA," she told MTV. "It was so unreal. It looks fake, like something out of a postcard... the video just shows this big landscape and the only person there is me."

Hot on its heels came 'Who's That Chick?', a David Guetta track on which Rihanna sang lead. It marked Rihanna's new position as ambassador for Doritos, and the snack company was involved in creating two videos – a day version featuring an angelic-looking Rihanna and a night version with a gothic persona. Meanwhile, the official promo, also featuring David Guetta, saw Rihanna dressed in candy-pink stockings and kitsch bright colours. Resembling a cross between a Disneyworld theme park and her friend Katy Perry's Candyland fantasies, it was about as far away from her former tough girl persona as it was possible to get.

To top it all, she started to refer to herself in the third person, commenting of herself, "She's awesome," and "The next stage in the revolution of Rihanna is perfect for us." In any other context, her multiple personae might have been branded a personality disorder worthy of psychiatric treatment, but in the pop world it seemed almost an obligatory rite of passage.

Beyoncé had an alter ego, an evil twin by the name of Sasha Fierce, who would be responsible for her sexier, fiercer side. According to Beyoncé, it only came out on special occasions – selected album releases being among these. However, while Beyoncé was good as gold in her day-to-day persona, Rihanna seemed to be naughty on an everyday basis. With that in mind, perhaps this more innocent, girly side to Rihanna was her shadow self – her rarely seen twin. But the fact that it was her angelic side that only made a rare appearance, rather than her more frequently seen devilish one, was part of why many fans loved her.

Meanwhile, her duet with Drake was released on October 29, 2010. It steadily climbed the charts, peaking at number one in both the USA and UK.

However, Rihanna didn't stay faithful to Drake for long – and the evidence of her infidelity was emblazoned across the world's TV screens. While the 'What's My Name?' video saw her cosying up to Drake on MTV on any given day, by November 6 she had switched teams and was flirting with Jon Bon Jovi instead. She made a surprise appearance at the MTV Europe Music Awards in Madrid for a pre-show event, leaping on stage to join him for the chorus of 'Livin' On A Prayer'.

Rihanna, who was wearing a crimson see-through dress, could be seen suggestively caressing his chest and making eyes at him in front of an astonished crowd of thousands. She also topped up her rock'n'roll credentials by sticking her tongue out at the camera and making finger gestures.

After getting Nuno Bettencourt on board, she had become highly sought after in the rock world – but she still found the attention immensely flattering. "When I found out Bon Jovi wanted me to sing with him, I flipped. I could not believe it," she exclaimed, before posting on Twitter "Wait! Did I just rock out with Bon Jovi last night?"

In contrast, *Loud* – which was released on November 16 – was a return to her signature sound, being the first album since *A Girl Like Me* to feature major dancehall and reggae influences. It was also a return to form, with slightly higher first week sales than any other album she had released. Evan had been concerned that *Rated R* might alienate the R&B market due to her sudden departure from the musical style that had gained her a fan base and, sure enough, it was the lowest performing album of her career – while sales were healthy, they didn't match that of *Good Girl Gone Bad*.

Loud was a different story. By December, her almost relentless chart presence saw three songs in the UK singles chart at the same time, with 'Only Girl In The World', 'What's My Name?' and 'Who's That Chick?' at numbers seven, eight and nine respectively.

The following month, she stepped up her game even further by joining Kanye West on 'All Of The Lights', a single released on January 18 for his fifth album, *My Beautiful Dark Twisted Fantasy*. Curiously, lyrics from Kanye included a reference to "doing time" for "slapping my girl". The song credits read like a chart rundown, including vocals from Alicia Keys, Fergie, Elton John, Kid Cudi – and of course, Rihanna herself.

But Rihanna wasn't just stopping at music. In her bid for world domination, she was also stepping up her efforts to create her own fashion line – according to rumours, a modern take on military-inspired chic.

Then she had diversified into art, releasing a book of photography entitled *The Last Girl On Earth*, in which her creative director Simon Henwood attempted to lift the lid on her secret world. The book was described as a "backstage pass" to the concept behind the tour, which itself was inspired by 1970s science fiction film *The Omega Man*. In the movie, biological warfare wipes out the entire population, seemingly leaving just one survivor. The lucky scientist has injected himself with a vaccine that protects him from poisons, but he discovers there are a few more inhabitants left in the world – and they are out to kill him. The movie follows his life in an apartment filled with firearms and explosives, dodging death until the end.

Although Rihanna had modelled her tour on the same theme, there would be one exception – she was a female superhero, so there would be a lot of good fashion. Parisian designer Alexandre Vauthier was involved in dressing her – someone who had turned down requests from Lady Gaga.

"He only works with people that fit in his world," Simon Henwood explained. "When it comes down to it, a designer wants the person that is wearing their work to bring it to life, not to use it like a costume, which is why he didn't dress Gaga."

The book followed Rihanna's journey of fashion, art and music – and battling the haters, of course – through to the final polished product, her world tour. It was a chance to show the "dark dream" that was her world behind the scenes, and pictures included Rihanna in cars, on video sets, in hotel rooms and even taking part in fashion shows.

While Rihanna's photo diary of the *Rated R* era sped around the world, she was already on the *Loud* campaign. In December, she performed on the final of *The X Factor* in the UK, joining Essex-born Matt Cardle – who would go on to win the show – for a duet of 'Unfaithful'. With the lithe, long-legged and statuesque Rihanna towering over him, Matt looked a little flustered, later confessing that he had a major crush on her. "I was actually thinking just, 'Don't get an erection!'" he confessed to MTV. "I had very thin, very soft trousers on and I was like 'please, please, please.' I was thinking 'Margaret Thatcher, Margaret Thatcher!'" However, the feeling wasn't reciprocated, with Rihanna laughing heartily at suggestions of a romance and dismissing him as "sweet".

In fact, the hot topic was not her chemistry with Matt, but her performance, which – complete with pelvic thrusts and suggestive dancing – took place before the 9 p.m. watershed. Taken together with burlesque routines from a scantily clad Christina Aguilera, the family show had parents squirming with embarrassment. Headlines in the *Daily Mail* screamed, "We don't need sex-crazed nymphs before the watershed." Meanwhile the following day, the paper published the offending screenshots with the words, "We apologise to readers, but you have to see these pictures to understand the fury they've caused."

A bemused Rihanna, who believed the performance had been erotic but not indecent, looked on as almost 3,000 complaints flooded into the programming regulator, Ofcom. A review later ruled that the scenes had not been inappropriate, but the outcry sparked a government-backed inquiry into pre-watershed programming. After recording 'Te Amo', Rihanna would have been aghast to learn that one of the changes called for was a ban on same-sex kissing on soaps or family TV shows.

But the ultimate censorship battle was yet to come.

Rihanna's next single, 'S&M', was instantly banned in 11 countries and didn't even make the playlist of Britain's top station, BBC Radio 1. Many stations, fearful of outraged listeners boycotting their shows for the explicit lyrics, added an edited version and renamed it 'Come On'.

Rihanna was furious. "'S&M' called 'Come On' now?" she tweeted. "Are you fucking kidding me?" The video received equally harsh treatment – a short, edited version was played on music channels during the day, with a full version not appearing until after the watershed.

However, one music channel, WTF TV, did dare to break the rules, airing 'S&M' at 11:25 in the morning. Ofcom responded by calling an emergency meeting. Complaints had been flooding in that the song was "completely unsuitable for daytime broadcast". WTF denied any pornographic element, claiming, "It is artistic and not dark or seedy." Yet, according to Ofcom, the video was dangerous for its repeated "focus on sex, bondage and sadomasochistic sexual practices", noting that some scenes could have "potentially dangerous consequences if imitated by children".

However, although *OK* magazine concurred that it was "every inch as red-hot, kinky and totally tongue in cheek as we expected it to be," Rihanna had a revelation to make – it wasn't about sex. "I am trying to deal with the criticism I got for dressing the way I did on 'Umbrella'," she explained. "For some people it was too shocking and too sexy. For me, it was totally natural to feel that way. With 'S&M', I am saying, 'I love that you hate my sexy side! Your hate gives me energy! I love it!'"

Director Melina Matsoukas confirmed, "It's about Rihanna's sadomasochistic relationship with the press – it isn't just about a bunch of whips and chains."

The video sampled those metaphors. First Rihanna is dragged to a press conference, struggling all the way, but ends up enjoying all the attention as she stands before a group of gagged journalists with newspaper headlines emblazoned on it. Later, members of the media are whipped and, in one of her most controversial scenes yet, she walks Perez Hilton – the outspoken gossip columnist who celebrities love to hate – on a dog leash. She also suggestively eats a banana, simulates sex with a doll and is photographed astride a table. For the banana shots, she requested a "spit bucket" between takes.

However, while it might all have been metaphorical, Rihanna was having a little too much fun on the shoot for it all to have been purely professional. According to a source, Rihanna and her best friend and assistant Melissa Forde had been indulging in some lesbian S&M action of their own behind the scenes.

"The stylist ordered in 15 gags for the dancers, but Rihanna grabbed them and started making her own photo shoot with Mel," the source explained. "She was pretending to whip her as they took pictures on their mobiles and she took a big bag of souvenirs home from the shoot."

What was more, one scene between Rihanna and a female dancer – which she had apparently initiated – was cut out of the video for being too sexy. She certainly wasn't afraid to push the boundaries.

She later revealed to *The Sun* that, even if 'S&M' had been a metaphor for relishing the negative attention lavished on her by the press, there was more of her in the character than she had previously admitted.

"I like to take the reins in my life, but be submissive in the bedroom," she let slip to *Rolling Stone*. "I love feeling like I'm somebody's girl. I love to be tied up and spanked... I can be a little lady and have a male who takes responsibility. That's sexy. I work hard and take a lot of decisions every day, so I prefer to feel the intimacy of someone like the girl."

She added, "I think I'm a bit masochistic. It's not something I'm proud of, and it's not something I noticed until recently. I think it's common for people who witness abuse in their household. They can never smell how beautiful a rose is unless they get pricked by a thorn."

She also revealed that she had forgiven her father for the behaviour that she believed had triggered her own craving to feel helpless at a lover's violence. "I actually feel really bad for my father," she explained. "He was abused too – he got beat up by his stepdad when he was young. He has resentment toward women, because he felt like his mom never protected him, and unfortunately, my mother was the victim of that. I'm not giving him excuses. Right is right and wrong is wrong. I still blame him. But I understand the source."

Meanwhile, if she wanted whips and chains from listeners too, she wouldn't have been disappointed. Scathing reviews were unleashed about the video, with American academic Diane Levin insisting that 'S&M' "promotes what I call 'compassion deficit disorder'. That is, it treats individuals as dehumanised objects, and sex and sexual behaviour out of the context of a caring human relationship – thereby undermining the foundation children need to grow up to have healthy relationships or sex."

However *PopJustice* defended Rihanna, countering, "It's not a pop star's job to babysit the nation's kids." Meanwhile, remembering her director's reassurance that all press was good press and that it was fantastic just to have them talking, she wasn't overly concerned.

While she might have appreciated the press, Rihanna wouldn't have loved all of the controversy – especially when she found herself sued. Stylist Ursula Stephen claimed that the creative input from Rihanna had been huge and that she had contributed "all kinds of crazy ideas". However, according to acclaimed fashion photographer David LaChapelle, the ideas were all his.

Radar Online was the first website to report the alleged copycat tactics, comparing the video to some of David's *Vogue Italia* fashion shoots. "In a side-by-side comparison between LaChapelle's previous work and screen captures of the music video, the similarities are indisputable, with nearly identical sets, scenarios and styling," it claimed. Within days, David had launched a lawsuit berating Rihanna and her director for directly copying the colours, themes, composition, lighting, styling, wardrobe and concept of eight of his pictures. He and Rihanna had worked together before and he knew her well, joking to *Radar*, "I think about her every time I get caught in the rain without my umbrella." But he wasn't about to get sentimental when it came to compensation – and the battle raged on.

Nevertheless – despite the bad press and the setback of having next-to-no video coverage or airplay during the peak listening hours – the song became a number one hit. Rihanna had an even bigger surprise for listeners in store when she asked fans which celebrity they would most like her to collaborate with. The answer by an overwhelming majority was Britney Spears. After a short and suspenseful silence, Rihanna premiered her very own 'RIH' mix of 'S&M', featuring none other than Britney herself. She tweeted the news that there was "a sexy collabo coming your way... it's Britney, bitch!" before Britney responded, "You're such a tease! I like it, like it..."

If the lyrical hints in Britney's tweets hadn't provided any clues, the speculation was over by April 11, when the remix hit the internet. "Britney never does features," Rihanna revealed proudly to New York radio station Z100. "It was really amazing that she really wanted to be a part of this song. She really liked the song to begin with, but it was a different story when she had to sing it and she really wanted to be a part of it. It made it really, really special because you never see two female pop artists doing songs together anymore." She added, "I hope [there'll be a video]. I want to spank Britney Spears!"

She wasn't the only person Rihanna wanted to spank. Taking some time out from her sexually submissive persona, she had also been spanking fellow singer Ke$ha in real life. Ke$ha, who saw Rihanna as a mentor, revealed, "She's so graceful and sweet and so badass. I saw her [recently] and she spanked me – always keeping me on my toes! She's the sickest."

Adding herself to the long list of people keen to collaborate with Rihanna – and perhaps to get a spanking on set – she added, "I don't know what she would be learning from me, aside from how to look like a maniac, but I definitely learned a lot from her."

However, not content with the stir 'S&M' had caused with its subsequent spanking scandals, Rihanna was soon on the lookout for a new single. She took to Twitter, asking fans to nominate their preferred track from 'Fading', 'Cheers (Drink To That)', 'California King Bed' and 'Man Down'. Although it was 'California King Bed' that had scored the highest, Rihanna couldn't resist making 'Man Down' a hit too, recording it as a US-only release.

She jetted off to the Jamaican capital of Kingston, which – dubbed the heart of gangland culture by many – provided the edgy atmosphere required for the video.

According to director Anthony Mandler, the plot she had in mind would seem shocking and intense – and he wasn't mistaken. Far from simply being a little inflammatory, it was a full-on scandal. Seconds into the video, Rihanna has pulled the trigger on a seemingly innocent victim, shooting him to his death in the middle of a crowded train station.

However, the mystery behind her anger is soon revealed when the video flashes back to Rihanna crying in the street following an implied rape. Trade the words 'sexual assault' for 'physical assault' and it seems to be a post-traumatic playback of her much-publicised altercation with Chris Brown. In the video, just as it had happened in real life, she had been flirting and chatting with her attacker just moments earlier – but when events took a sinister turn for the worst, Rihanna was left alone and vulnerable in the road.

The video depicting Rihanna's brutal revenge attack was released to the American public on May 3, 2011. Yet would impressionable younger fans who had also been assaulted copy Rihanna's fictional story by taking the law into their own hands? That was the question on many people's lips.

According to Paul Porter, co-founder of the organisation Industry Ears, which vets potentially harmful media images, the fact that Rihanna had been abused was no excuse for her response. "If Chris Brown shot a woman in his new video, the world would stop," he claimed in a public statement. "Rihanna should not get a pass." He added that in the 30 years he had run his company, he had "never witnessed such a cold, calculated execution of murder in prime time".

Indeed, while the authorities might have been willing to ignore the song when it was tucked away surreptitiously on her album, there would be no chance of that when it was accompanied by a provocative video on prime-time TV. The *Parents' Television Council* also came forward to argue that the video advocated "premeditated murder" as retaliation for a crime and made it seem acceptable. This was in spite of the fact that Rihanna had expressed regret for losing her 'cool' in the lyrics.

Yet director Anthony Mandler was unapologetic. He had wanted a video that matched 'Russian Roulette' in the controversy stakes and, given his past history with Rihanna on the music video scene, that might have seemed a tall order. However, he felt he had succeeded, describing the outcome as "dramatic and shocking and intense and emotional and uplifting and enlightening".

He felt the industry had been crying out for more brave, no-holds-barred depiction of real-life situations, no matter how gory, and he name-checked Aerosmith's 'Janie's Got A Gun' as one of his inspirations.

He also added to MTV, "It's my favourite song she's ever recorded... it's just one of those songs that demands a strong narrative and visual and let's just say she let me go all the way."

It might also have seemed unfair that other fatal gunshot moments in music had been left unchecked. For example, in the liberated 1960s, Jimi Hendrix's 'Hey Joe' – which depicts a man shooting down his unfaithful wife – seemed to have passed censors without a single query. Yet in modern times, Rihanna was facing the full force of media scrutiny.

She was defiant, too. To her, she was simply being a voice for young people, daring to say the things that other pseudo-squeaky clean artists were afraid to talk about with honesty. In an MTV interview, she insisted that this was "art with a message" and without barriers.

She then tweeted a series of defensive messages, claiming, "I'm a 23-year-old rockstar with *no kids*! What's up with everybody wanting me to be a parent? I'm just a girl, I can only be your/our voice! Because we all know how difficult/embarrassing it is to communicate touchy subject matters with anyone, especially your parents! And this is why! Because we turn the other cheek! You can't hide your kids from society, or they'll never learn how to adapt! This is the *real world*!"

But Chris Brown no longer needed to be quaking in his boots at the prospect of cold-blooded murder, when she finally revealed to Black Entertainment TV, "I've been abused in the past and you don't see me running around killing people in my spare time!"

Chris might now be able to breathe a huge sigh of relief, but for Rihanna the pressure was unrelenting. This was the second single in a row that would attract widespread criticism – and while all the attention might have been satisfying at first, continually explaining herself was quickly becoming trying.

However, Anthony Mandler was on her team and was delighted that she had joined him in his quest for full-on controversy. "It's doing exactly what Rihanna and I hoped it would do, which is shine a light on the very dark subject matter... the fact that there's an argument to ban this because it will make girls retaliate from abuse with murder is skipping over the point," he told *The Hollywood Reporter*. "We obviously have a huge issue to deal with as a country."

179

He added that modern artists were 'wasting' an opportunity to give messages about the wrongs of society through music videos, citing Madonna's early straight-talking as an inspiration. He also added teasingly that he and Rihanna had held back from making the video as dramatic as they had originally wanted it to be, and so were surprised it had sparked offence.

In another intriguing twist, a famous rape victim also joined the debate. The *Cadillac Records* actress Gabrielle Union stepped in to defend Rihanna's video, revealing on Twitter that aged just 19, she had shot at a stranger after being raped during a burglary. "During my rape, I tried to shoot my rapist, but I missed," she tweeted. "Over the years I realised that killing my rapist would've added insult to injury. The desire to kill someone who abused/raped you is understandable, but unless it's self-defence on the moment to save your life, [it] just adds to your troubles."

However, she praised 'Man Down', claiming that the video "did a great job of getting the entire world talking about rape! U hope that it leads to healing and prevents rape."

Rihanna herself had a similar story to tweet, insisting that the video's message to young people was that they should be careful to avoid violence and empower themselves by using forethought. "Young girls/women all over the world… we are a lot of things!" she wrote. "We're strong, innocent, fun, flirtatious, vulnerable and sometimes our innocence can cause us to be naïve! We always think it could *never* be us, but in reality it can happen to *any* of us! So ladies, be careful!"

As much as Rihanna had fought against being a parent figure and a role model, she seemed to be becoming one – and hopefully to great effect. Plus she had proved to fans that disaster could happen to anyone, as she revealed in the CNN interview about her assault recorded two years earlier. She had said that, due to her revulsion at seeing her mother get battered, she had always thought she would never allow herself to fall prey to the same fate – until she fell in love. She'd wanted to prove that anyone, no matter how famous, self-confident or successful, was immune. To her, it was a matter of a disease called love – and that could affect anyone.

She also denied the accusations that the video would inspire young victims to kill. She claimed that the murder in 'Man Down' was in fact a metaphor for killing a lover by breaking his heart. To her, the pain of a love affair coming to an end was just as real and authentic as a genuine gunshot. It didn't sound as though she was merely covering her back with that interpretation either – she'd already flirted with life and death metaphors for romance in 'Unfaithful', where she sang that putting a gun to her lover's head would be kinder than prolonging the agony he will experience when he learns that she has been untrue.

However, despite her denials, Rihanna admitted being seduced by the glamorous 'gangsta vibe' of 'Man Down', suggesting that she was proud of the real-life references to shooting after all. "'Man Down' is gangsta," she revealed jubilantly to MTV. "It comes from me trying to achieve that vibe."

Although Rihanna had experimented with numerous musical styles in her career, her subsequent comments, delivered in a strong West Indian accent, left no uncertainty about where her loyalties lay. She was flying the flag for the Caribbean. "I'm super inspired by reggae music," she claimed. "I grew up listening to it. I grew up loving it. My favourite artists are all reggae artists." Defending 'Man Down' still further, she added, "The special thing in that song is the fact that it's a female singing those lyrics, then you have that reggae thing and the chant; the overall energy in that song is so gangsta... it's got a lot of swagger."

That sentiment wasn't lost on the *Los Angeles Times*, which reviewed the single by saying, "'Man Down' reasserts her Caribbean lilt with a swaggering murder ballad that one can't help but hear as a warning shot across the radio dial to Chris Brown's 'Deuces.'"

All the drama certainly spelt publicity. Within a week of its release, the video had already attracted over 12 million views on YouTube. Yet a poor chart performance followed, with actual sales leading to a measly peak of just 61 on the US *Billboard* Hot 100 chart, although it fared better on the Hot R&B/Hip Hop Songs chart with a high of 13.

Some onlookers speculated that the strong, vengeful tone of the song might have ultimately alienated listeners after an initial surge of interest caused by shock value. Others countered that the strong West Indian accent and non-Western sound might have been responsible. Perhaps that was the case – after all, hadn't ex-Combermere ally Paul Browne expressed his concern that, although reggae was huge in Barbados, it might struggle to hold a large audience worldwide? Yet Rihanna had stuck to her guns and stayed true to her instincts – and, for the most part, her loyal fan base had responded positively.

Ironically however, while some people were outraged by the audacity of Rihanna, who had quickly become a scandal magnet, others were arguing that she wasn't being controversial enough. While 'Man Down' stormed the airwaves in the USA, the rest of the world had to be content with 'California King Bed', a softer number with almost country music elements, which depicted the ending of a relationship between two lovers who had gradually become emotionally estranged.

Some disappointed European fans declared the decision a cop-out, longing for the boundary-breaking Rihanna they knew and loved. They saw 'California King Bed' as a tame alternative, arguing that a song as risqué as 'Man Down' represented Rihanna as an artist – someone who had built her image on defying society's norms and who'd never been afraid to be a risk-taker. It seemed that she couldn't win – she was either offensively controversial or lame and just not controversial enough.

Fans might have craved something as straight-talking as her 'cold-blooded murder' tune – to their pleasure, not exactly a traditional love sonnet – but according to Anthony Mandler, who also directed the video for 'California King Bed', she was simply showing another side to herself. "She wanted to obviously show a softer side, a lighter side… there's so much variety with her," he told MTV. "Whatever character she's playing, whatever side of herself she's showing, she's in it 1,000 percent."

Taking a chance to do something different paid off. Following its release on May 13, the track peaked at number eight in the UK, number four in Australia and number five in New Zealand among others.

However, it wasn't long before she irritated some of her fans yet again – this time by starting a dialogue with Chris Brown. The restraining order that bound them to an agreement not to go near each other had expired on February 22, in time for both to perform at the Grammys, but was there more to it than that? Either way, the pair had begun communicating again.

Gossip magazines such as *Heat* claimed that they had met secretly at New York hotels such as the Gansevoort, rumours which gained a little more currency in readers' eyes when they discovered the two had signed up to follow each other on Twitter. The move was initiated by Rihanna, shortly after the release of 'California King Bed', leading to feverish speculation that she was still love-struck. Chris had reciprocated her attentions by sending his ex-lover a message on the website, asking, "You got that picture I sent you?"

Fans had replied in their droves to express their indignation. One wrote, "I never thought you would go back to him! You better not, it's your life but you do have people that look up to you, e.g. young girls," forcing Rihanna to defensively respond, "It's fucking Twitter, not the altar! Calm down." She then had a change of heart, posting the apology, "Babygirl I'm sorry, I didn't mean to hurt or offend u! Just needed to make it clear…"

Some speculated Chris had ulterior motives in befriending Rihanna, trying to garner support by seeming to have been forgiven for the assault just in time to publicise his upcoming single 'Beautiful People'. Others felt that he was trying to rekindle a romance with her and that, due to how quickly the attack had brought their relationship crashing down, they might still have unfinished business.

MTV seemed to add fuel to the fire when its Canadian website reported on a Twitter message she had allegedly written, saying, "I admit it. I provoked Chris [Brown] to hit me. It's not entirely his fault. I'm sorry." An infuriated Rihanna instantly took to Twitter to set the record straight. "Are you fucking kidding me?" she exclaimed. "You're supposed to be a reliable source for news on music and this is the bullshit you post?"

Perhaps it wasn't surprising Rihanna was feeling sensitive. A new lawsuit was being filed against her by photographer Philipp Paulus who claimed, like David LaChapelle before him, that Rihanna had plagiarised images he had made for the magazine *Paperworld* in the video 'S&M'. His attorney released a statement declaring his action in no uncertain terms. "Copyright laws of our client have been infringed and the worldwide million-wise exploitation of the video 'S&M' is unlawful… [and] Paulus will take legal action against Rihanna," it read.

Paulus then raged in an interview with *Radar*, "Why a worldwide celebrity is not able to afford a creative director, who creates individual concepts and stagings, is incomprehensible to me… To create new things within the creative cosmos, you can only expect this to come from a real genius, there is no doubt about it. In this case, there is no real genius who created their own work; instead they stole ideas from a creative talent. Furthermore, every other creative professional should realise how supremely embarrassing it is to copy the work of colleagues from the artistic world and then to be praised for it."

If she hadn't been embarrassed up until then, she certainly would be now. To add to that, there was the drama with Chris, something that she hoped to have put behind her a long time ago. As if to symbolise all of the strife, Rihanna then fell to her knees in front of 16,000 people when she tripped on her heels performing 'What's My Name?', at the Rexall Place Arena in Edmonton, Canada, on June 22.

However, whether Rihanna's status with Chris was now that of a friend, acquaintance or lover, she seemed to have moved on from the trauma of the attack – and in spite of the hiccups with the media and run-ins with the law, her career was moving forward in leaps and bounds.

Meanwhile, Rihanna had also collaborated a second time with Nicki Minaj on the song 'Scared To Be Beautiful'. Ironically for someone who'd been blessed with model looks, Rihanna – like Lady Gaga – still found beautiful "boring". Not only did she have the desire to be edgy and risqué instead of pretty and feminine, but she also had her own insecurities too – which she wanted to share with impressionable younger fans to demonstrate that, underneath the diva status, she suffered from body issues just like them. Even a team of stylists – who Rihanna frequently joked had "tricked" the world into thinking she looked "hot" – couldn't remove the occasional twinge of insecurity.

"The lyrics to that song are about a young girl who removes the mirrors from her house because she cannot bear to look at herself. That really happens," she explained. "I hate that girls grow up that way. I have my own issues under this skirt. Cellulite is a reality for me, like most women. I really used to worry about my thighs but I have learnt to accept the shape I am."

In the past, Rihanna had always wanted to outwardly exude confidence and toughness, not wanting her enemies to see that she was vulnerable. However, her ultimate strength had become not being afraid to be confessional and expose her fears, realising it didn't make her a lesser person. For her, that was the real symbol of toughness – coming out and admitting that at times she wasn't. She didn't want fans to see an airbrushed image of perfection and then worry about themselves. She wanted to be transparent about her own issues so that – as she grew in confidence – her fans could grow along with her.

There had previously been concern that Rihanna was anorexic, particularly when interviews yielded headlines such as "Carbs are the enemy." Despite having tales to tell of a draconically strict exercise-and-diet regime and a phobia of high-fat foods, by 2011 Rihanna definitely had her confidence back. On learning that model Kate Moss had told the world, "Nothing tastes as good as skinny feels," she shrieked 'hysterically' in indignation, telling *News Of the World,* "I can't believe she said that. That is so crazy. I love food because I'm from Barbados." She added, "If I was a catwalk model, I'd be considered fat which I know is ridiculous."

To demonstrate her heightened body confidence, Rihanna had broken her promise never to pose naked again, appearing nude and natural for Nivea's 100-year anniversary campaign.

Not only did Rihanna have added confidence, she was also at the top of her game financially. She'd purchased a £7 million home in LA's exclusive Bel Air community, with famous neighbours like Lady Gaga nearby.

The 10,000 square foot property contained a dance floor, private cinema, luxury built-in spa, swimming pool, sauna, steam room, extensive library and large open-plan balconies. There were also walk-in wardrobes where her large shoe collection took pride of place. It boasted eight bedrooms and 12 bathrooms.

The detached property was also a guaranteed party hotspot due to its secluded location – Rihanna could pump up the volume on her days off without fear of offending disgruntled neighbours. It was a far cry from the past when she was teased from singing in the shower in Barbados.

Rihanna had credentials too – with Britney and Nicki Minaj collaborations under her belt, she had also been into the studio to record new songs with Katy Perry. However, there was one collaboration planned which she hoped would put an end to any rumours of bad blood once and for all – Beyoncé.

A source had made fresh accusations to *Look* magazine that Rihanna was a factor in an alleged breakdown of Beyoncé's marriage to Jay-Z. "Beyoncé feels Jay spends a lot of time mentoring Rihanna," the source claimed. "Rihanna gets a lot of sexy songs which would be guaranteed hits for Beyoncé, but I think she feels she doesn't even get a look in because Jay doesn't want people looking at his wife in that way."

However, gossip stirrers were eating their words when it was reported that Rihanna and Beyoncé had hit the studio – together. The secret duet would be appearing on Beyoncé's next studio album.

However, in spite of all her successes since the incident with Chris Brown, it was still imperative for Rihanna that people didn't judge her by that night. Her signature scent, Rebel Flower, was the icing on the cake to change all that. Not only had Rihanna had the words "*rebelle fleur*" tattooed on her neck to cement her status as a beautiful but tough superstar, she'd also helped with research to find the perfect fragrance worthy of putting her name on.

"Over the years, I layered many different scents to get something that was truly my own," she explained of the perfume. "But I wanted something that said, 'Rihanna was here.' Something delicious and special, a fragrance with subtle hints that linger and leave a sexy memory."

The memories had no chance of not being sexy – the adverts to promote the scent featured her skin being caressed by several anonymous male hands. The fragrance also represented her childhood memories – the fruits and floral scents that were synonymous with her Caribbean roots, as well as vanilla and amber undertones to add sex appeal.

Far from being seen as a victim, Rihanna was hoping to leave just one statement behind, one that no-one would dare to question – the lingering scent of a rebel.